Rethinking Cyberlaw

RETHINKING LAW

The *Rethinking Law* series is a forum for innovative scholarly legal writing from across all substantive fields of law. The series aims to enrich the study of law by promoting a cutting-edge approach to legal analysis.

Despite the old maxim that nothing is new under the sun, it is nevertheless true that laws evolve and contexts in which laws operate change. Law faces new and previously unforeseen challenges, responds to shifting motivations and is shaped by competing interests and experiences. Academic scrutiny and challenge is an essential component in the development of law, and the act of re-thinking and re-examining principles and precepts that may have been long-held is imperative.

Rethinking Law showcases authored books that address their field from a new angle, expose the weaknesses of existing frameworks, or 're-frame' the topic in some way. This might be through the introduction of a new legal framework, through the integration of perspectives from other fields or even other disciplines, through challenging existing paradigms, or simply through a level of analysis that elevates or sharpens our understanding of a subject. While each book takes its own approach, all the titles in the series use an analytical lens to open up new thinking.

Titles in the series include:

Rethinking Contract Law and Contract Design
Victor P. Goldberg

Rethinking Cyberlaw
A New Vision for Internet Law
Jacqueline Lipton

Rethinking Cyberlaw

A New Vision for Internet Law

Jacqueline Lipton

David L. Brennan Chair in Law and Director, Center for Intellectual Property Law and Technology, University of Akron School of Law, USA

RETHINKING LAW

Edward Elgar PUBLISHING

Cheltenham, UK • Northampton, MA, USA

Published by
Edward Elgar Publishing Limited
The Lypiatts
15 Lansdown Road
Cheltenham
Glos GL50 2JA
UK

Edward Elgar Publishing, Inc.
William Pratt House
9 Dewey Court
Northampton
Massachusetts 01060
USA

A catalogue record for this book
is available from the British Library

Library of Congress Control Number: 2014952140

This book is available electronically in the **Elgar**online
Law subject collection
DOI 10.4337/9781781002186

MIX
Paper from responsible sources
FSC® C013056

ISBN 978 1 78100 217 9 (cased)
ISBN 978 1 78100 218 6 (eBook)

Typeset by Columns Design XML Ltd, Reading
Printed and bound in Great Britain by T.J. International Ltd, Padstow

Contents

Acknowledgments

As with any project that spans multiple years, it takes a village to support the author and I am grateful to have had the support of so many colleagues, friends and law school administrators over the years it took me to conceptualize and complete this book. The ideas that later became the backbone of the book were first workshopped in a roundtable generously organized and funded by the Fordham Law School's Center on Law and Information Policy. My special thanks go to Professor Joel Reidenberg and Jamela Debelak for making this event possible.

The administrations at the Case Western Reserve University School of Law and the University of Houston Law Center were especially supportive of my work and, in particular, I would like to thank Interim Dean Robert Rawson, Dean Raymond Nimmer, and Interim Dean Richard Alderman for supporting this project. Invaluable research assistance was provided by Yusra Khalid at the University of Houston Law Center. My colleagues in the Institute for Intellectual Property and Information Law at the University of Houston Law Center were also wonderfully supportive: Professors Craig Joyce, Greg Vetter, Sapna Kumar, and Paul Janicke. Thanks also to my new colleagues at the University of Akron School of Law for their support: Interim Dean Elizabeth Reilly, Dean Matthew Wilson, and Professor Ryan Vacca in particular.

Thanks to Professor Peter Yu for continuing to involve me in his work with Edward Elgar, and special thanks to all the staff at Edward Elgar who have worked on this book and my previous book, *Internet Domain Name, Trademarks, and Free Speech*. Tara Gorvine has worked with me in developing both book proposals and seen the projects through to fruition and I'm hoping we can work together again in the future. My sincere thanks also to Chloe Mitchell for the terrific job on editing this manuscript.

So many friends and colleagues have helped me over the years with this project that I know I'll omit someone if I try to list them all, but I'm going to do my best. Apologies if the list is necessarily incomplete, but for what it's worth, my heartfelt thanks go to: Professors Jessica Litman, David Post, Leah Chan Grinvald, Edward Lee, Cynthia Ho, Mary Wong (now at ICANN), Elizabeth Rowe, Irina Manta, James Grimmelman,

Nancy Kim, Margaret Chon, Susan Scafidi, Sharona Hoffman, Cassandra Robertson, Derek Bambauer, Raymond Ku, Gaia Bernstein, and Andrea Matwyshyn.

On the personal level, as always my thanks go to my family for supporting my work. All my love and thanks to Patrick, Sean, Brianne and Megan.

July 2, 2014

1. The scope of cyberlaw

1.1 RECONSIDERING CYBERLAW

1.1.1 The Nature of Cyberlaw

Since the explosion of the Internet into our daily lives in the mid- to late 1990s, scholars have struggled with the question as to whether the omnipresence of this global communications medium has – or should be regarded as having – given rise to a new legal field.[1] While cyberlaw courses have become a staple in law school curricula, there is little consensus as to what the subject might – or should – entail. A frequent argument against cyberlaw is that there is no "there" there: in other words, cyberlaw is merely the collation of a loosely related set of cases and principles from various fields of law that happen to involve the Internet.[2]

Some commentators have argued that, even if this is true, cyberlaw can still teach us important lessons about the nature of legal regulation, as contrasted with other regulatory modalities. For example, Professors Lessig and Reidenberg have forcefully argued that cyberlaw is an important conceptual field within which to contrast the nature of law as a regulator of human conduct against other regulatory modalities, notably system architecture, or software code. These scholars have suggested that the latter, particularly code, are likely much more effective in terms of constraining what people can and cannot do online than legal regulation.[3]

This book reconsiders the question of the nature of cyberlaw with the benefit of hindsight. While earlier scholars considered the questions

---

[1] See, for example, Frank Easterbrook, *Cyberspace and the Law of the Horse*, 1996 U. CHI. LEGAL F. 207 (1996); Lawrence Lessig, *The Law of the Horse: What Cyberlaw Might Teach*, 113 HARV. L. REV. 501 (1999) [hereinafter, *What Cyberlaw Might Teach*]; Raymond Ku, *A Brave New Cyberworld?*, 22 T. JEFFERSON L. REV. 125 (2000).

[2] Easterbrook, *supra* note 1.

[3] LAWRENCE LESSIG, CODE 2.0 (2006); Joel Reidenberg, *Lex Informatica: The Formulation of Information Policy Rules through Technology*, 76 TEXAS L. REV. 553 (1998).

prospectively – in terms of how the Internet *might* impact human behavior and how courts and legislatures might respond to online problems, this book considers these questions looking back on roughly fifteen to twenty years of legal developments in response to the Internet. On the basis of existing case law and legislation, it attempts to draw common threads from situations dealing with issues as facially diverse as defamation; privacy; protection of intellectual property rights; fraud, identity theft and other forms of cyber-victimization; and questions of information ownership and access.

The knowledge we now possess about how cyberspace has in fact been regulated helps to answer questions as to what the cyberlaw field should ideally look like. The dual aims of this book are to: (a) justify the existence of cyberlaw as a legal field; and (b) describe how it might be framed as a more cohesive field of study than has previously been the case. The ability to reframe cyberlaw in light of the realities of modern regulation will aid the development of the field in more pragmatic and predictable directions.

1.1.2 Central Tenets of Cyberlaw as a Law of the Intermediated Information Exchange

This book argues that several forces can unify cyberlaw, revolving round the fact that the Internet is, at its core, an interactive global online communications system. This deceptively simple fact speaks to the heart of what is unique about regulating online conduct. Because the Internet is a communications medium, all online transactions involve the exchange of *information* between individuals rather than physical interactions between them. Thus the regulation of information exchange must be a central feature of Internet law. The extent to which information can be propertized – or commodified – is a very significant factor in this equation. The lack of *physical interaction* online means that Internet law deals entirely with intangible property.

Along with the importance of *information* as a central tenet of cyberlaw, all online interactions involve the participation of one or more *intermediaries* – organizations that enable digital information exchange. These intermediaries range from Internet Service Providers (ISPs) that enable basic access to forums for specific kinds of information exchange such as search engines, online social networks, electronic retailers/ auction sites, data aggregators, blogs, educational institutions, and government departments. In many ways, cyberlaw is the law of third-party-mediated information exchanges. Thus, the central focus of a reconceptualized cyberlaw field should be on issues involving regulation of information, and on the role of these intermediaries within information exchanges.

1.1.3 Common Themes Underlying Cyberlaw: Jurisdiction, Norms and Harms

Outside of these two key concepts – the central role of *information* and *intermediaries* – come other distinctive questions related to online conduct. These questions may not be as unique to cyberlaw as the foundational tenets of information and intermediaries. However, they are significant enough to comprise what we might think of as common themes underlying much of the field. The main common themes of cyberlaw revolve around: (a) the global reach of the Internet; (b) differing norms of behavior that occur online as compared with those in the physical world; and, (c) the kinds of harms suffered as a result of undesirable online behavior. Each of these aspects of the Internet can prove challenging for regulators and they are all somewhat interrelated.

The fact that much Internet content can be accessed simultaneously in most countries raises jurisdictional challenges along with the specter of differing cultural norms that may come into conflict in terms of attitudes to appropriate regulation. What is a matter of free speech in the United States may not be protected elsewhere, either normatively or as a matter of constitutional law. Outside problems of cultural norm divergence are potential divergences of social norms between online communities: for example, what may be acceptable in an adult chatroom may not be acceptable on a child-friendly blog. Additionally, online and offline norms within similar communities may vary.

It has been well documented that people interacting online tend to be much less inhibited with a lesser tendency to self-censor than people interacting in the real world.[4] Part of the reason for this may be the absence of physical world cues online that impact conduct in the real world, including facial expressions, tones of voice and body language. All of these subtle cues are missing from online interactions. When confronted with a computer monitor rather than a person, people tend to be disinhibited in their conduct.

---

[4] See, for example, SHERRY TURKLE, ALONE TOGETHER: WHY WE EXPECT MORE FROM TECHNOLOGY AND LESS FROM EACH OTHER, 235–36 (2011) (describing the way that individuals often respond to each other in much more coarse and aggressive ways online than in physical space).

Internet-based harms also raise challenges different in scope and nature than their physical world counterparts. The harms engendered by, say, intellectual property infringement or defamation online may be much greater in scope and scale than their physical world analogs because of the global reach of Internet communications. The Internet also raises the specter of new classes of harm engendered by flame wars,[5] global privacy or reputation damage, and widespread anonymous vigilante justice.[6] The ability to aggregate information online quickly and easily from multiple sources and to distribute it at the push of a button can cause much more comprehensive and global damage to an individual in terms of cyber-harassment and cyber-bullying than was ever possible in the physical world.[7]

To the extent that the Internet enables new kinds of harm, or at least harms on a more aggregated global scale, the field of cyberlaw will ultimately also be faced with new questions involving appropriate legal remedies for these harms. Injunctive relief may be more appropriate in most cases than monetary relief. Injunctive relief will tend to impact online intermediaries more significantly than perhaps those individuals who participate in harmful information exchanges. Imposing injunctions on intermediaries to stanch harmful information flows will be much more effective than seeking relief against individuals often in multiple jurisdictions. However, this approach will also raise questions about appropriate legal burdens to impose on intermediaries in terms of monitoring and controlling the conduct of those who utilize their services. This book will examine a number of case studies involving the balance of legal rights and responsibilities imposed on intermediaries in fields such as copyright infringement, trademark infringement, privacy, defamation and cyber-harassment.

1.2 WHAT MIGHT "NOT" BE CYBERLAW

An attempt to identify the boundaries and unifying themes of cyberlaw also necessitates a consideration of what might not belong within those boundaries, at least as central tenets or common themes. If cyberlaw is regarded as the law of the intermediated information exchange, some

---

[5] *Id.* (discussing concerns about online flaming and flame wars).

[6] Jacqueline Lipton, *"We, the Paparazzi": Developing a Privacy Paradigm for Digital Video*, 95 IOWA LAW REVIEW 919, 921–22 (2010) (providing examples of online vigilante justice) [hereinafter, *Paparazzi*].

[7] *Id.*

issues become more peripheral to the field than existing casebooks and syllabi would suggest. These issues include regulation of the hardware through which online communications take place, and some of the more procedural jurisdictional questions. This sub-section examines why these issues, while undoubtedly relevant to the study of cyberlaw, should not be regarded as a central focus of the field.

In terms of the hardware – the pipes, cables and bandwidth that enable online communications – it is true that these elements of the system will be subject to legal regulation. Nevertheless the regulation of the infrastructure is largely a separate question to regulating the content passing through the system (except perhaps in debates about network neutrality). The regulation of network infrastructure is a highly specialized and government-specific aspect of the Internet. While a content-based cyberlaw course is relatively generalized, focusing on the global regulation of online conduct and content, the regulation of telecommunications hardware is an extremely sophisticated and jurisdiction-specific endeavor. While the two are related, it is too difficult, and largely unnecessary, to include the infrastructure regulation piece as part of a cyberlaw course, except perhaps to touch on it as an issue important in its own right but not necessarily central to the basic course of study.

Many existing cyberlaw texts also devote some time to procedural conflicts of law issues which are again a highly specialized and highly jurisdiction-specific area of the law. These issues could safely be relegated to the sidelines in cyberlaw courses of the future for the following reasons. While in the early days of the Internet, questions arose as to whether cyberspace was a new jurisdictional "place" (for want of a better term)[8] that was not amenable to existing conflicts of law principles, these questions have largely been resolved in practice in the negative. Courts have not been reticent to impose existing conflicts principles in cyberspace, particularly in the realm of personal jurisdiction.[9]

---

[8] Dan Hunter, *Cyberspace as Place and the Tragedy of the Digital Anticommons*, 91 CALIFORNIA L. REV. 439 (2003) (discussing cognitive developmental reasons why we employ real place metaphors to describe cyberspace).

[9] Examples in the United States are: *Bensusan Restaurant v King*, 937 F. Supp. 297 (S.D.N.Y. 1996); *aff'd* 126 F.3d 25 (ed. Cir 1997); *Inset Systems v Instruction Set*, 937 F. Supp. 161 (D. Conn. 1996); *Zippo Manufacturing v Zippo Dot Com*, 952 F. Supp. 1119 (W.D. Pa. 1997); *Compuserve v Patterson*, 89 F.3d 1257 (1996); *Origins v Kotler*, 133 F. Supp. 2d 1232 (D.N.M. 2001); *Bochan v La Fontaine*, 68 F. Supp. 2d 692 (E.D. Va. 1999); *Oasis v Judd*, 132 F. Supp. 2d

Some litigants have expressed concern that subjecting foreign defendants to an unfamiliar jurisdiction could lead to the unfair imposition of unanticipated and expensive legal consequences for an online communication published generally to the world at large.[10] However, judges have been generally unsympathetic to these arguments, noting that defendants should know when their online conduct could raise problems in a foreign jurisdiction and should take appropriate action to avoid liability. For example, in the famous *Gutnick v Dow Jones* case,[11] the High Court of Australia noted that Dow Jones knew that their online publication was available in Australia, where the plaintiff would suffer the brunt of the defamation. They affirmatively chose to make the publication available to Australian subscribers, and the Australian courts and laws were thus appropriate for the case. In the *Yahoo!* case involving La Ligue Contre Le Racisme,[12] a French court granted an injunction to prevent Yahoo! customers from selling Nazi memorabilia to French customers on the basis that even though Yahoo! could not absolutely ensure that no such memorabilia was ever sold to a French customer, it could employ some relatively effective mechanisms to prevent the sales.[13]

---

612 (S.D. Ohio 2001); *Chang v Virgin Mobile USA, LLC*, 2009 WL 111570 (N.D.Tex. January 16, 2009).

[10] See, for example, *Dow Jones v Gutnick*, [2002] HCA 56, para. 165 ("The notion that those who publish defamatory material on the Internet are answerable before the courts of any nation where the damage to reputation has occurred, such as in the jurisdiction where the complaining party resides, presents difficulties: technological, legal and practical. It is true that the law of Australia provides protections against some of those difficulties which, in appropriate cases, will obviate or diminish the inconvenience of distant liability. Moreover, the spectre of 'global' liability should not be exaggerated. Apart from anything else, the costs and practicalities of bringing proceedings against a foreign publisher will usually be a sufficient impediment to discourage even the most intrepid of litigants. Further, in many cases of this kind, where the publisher is said to have no presence or assets in the jurisdiction, it may choose simply to ignore the proceedings. It may save its contest to the courts of its own jurisdiction until an attempt is later made to enforce there the judgment obtained in the foreign trial. It may do this especially if that judgment was secured by the application of laws, the enforcement of which would be regarded as unconstitutional or otherwise offensive to a different legal culture").

[11] *Id.*

[12] *Ligue Contre Le Racisme et L'Antisemitisme v Yahoo!*, Superior Ct. of Paris (Nov. 20, 2000).

[13] *Id.*

In other words, jurisdiction does not appear to have become the problem it was initially believed to be. Obviously, a global communications medium potentially causes a greater number of cross-border legal issues, but that fact has not prevented the application of conflicts principles to cases where Internet conduct is implicated. It is possible that a greater number of Internet-related cases are effectively resolved at the jurisdictional stage and that courts do not get a chance to rule on substantive legal issues as often as they do in non-Internet cases involving multiple jurisdictions. However, there is no empirical evidence available to decisively support this argument. As with questions relating to the regulation of the hardware, conflicts of law principles are highly specialized and jurisdiction-specific. While they are relevant to the study of cyberlaw, they should not be regarded as comprising its central focus. What we can learn from cyberlaw as a cohesive field relates to the regulation of intermediated conduct involving online content, rather than the application of specific conflicts principles in given cases.

Another aspect of cyberspace regulation that has also taken up significant space in cyberlaw casebooks to date – and perhaps could now be relegated to a position of lesser importance – is the question of legislative competence of domestic governments to regulate online conduct. As with conflicts questions, these issues have not proved to present major hurdles for Internet regulation despite concerns raised about lack of domestic legislative competence over "virtual places" in the early days of the Internet. Domestic governments have effectively regulated much online conduct in the ensuing years. The one exception may be laws that implicate First Amendment concerns in the United States,[14] and perhaps some commerce clause issues.[15]

While the debate about whether cyberspace should be subject to domestic regulation has pretty much been answered in the affirmative, the question of the most effective approaches to Internet regulation remains a significant facet of cyberlaw in terms of policy debates about regulation more generally. As noted above, Internet regulation will *always* involve one or more online intermediaries facilitating information transactions. Thus, an important question for cyberlaw should be the extent to which laws should be focused on intermediaries, rather than primary actors. Another important question for cyberspace regulation

---

[14] See, for example, *Reno v ACLU*, 521 U.S. 844 (1997); *Aschcroft v ACLU*, 535 U.S. 564 (2002).

[15] See, for example, *American Libraries Association v Pataki*, 969 F. Supp. 160 (S.D.N.Y. 1997).

going forward will be identifying areas where legal regulation is important as opposed to other forms of regulation – such as software code, market forces and social norms.[16] The interplay between these regulatory modalities is also an important question. Legal regulation does not operate in a vacuum and it is important to examine ways in which laws support other regulatory modalities and vice versa. For example, in areas where social norms are underdeveloped laws may serve a significant expressive function outside their potential for enforcement.[17]

The global nature of the Internet also creates a need for legislatures to consider the extent to which global harmonization is desirable. Currently there are some significant global disjoints between approaches to the regulation of online privacy, defamation, and to some extent even intellectual property law. The recent Google privacy issues in the European Union are a clear example of this lack of harmonization. The European Union effectively requires Google to delete certain records about an individual from search results while the United States laws do not require similar action.[18] Lack of harmonization can lead to confusion and expense, difficulties relating to cross-border enforcement, and the temptation of powerful countries to exert political pressure on less powerful countries to bring their laws into compliance.

1.3 DEFINING KEY TERMS: *INFORMATION* AND *INTERMEDIARY*

1.3.1 Information

As noted above, as an intermediated communications medium, the regulation of the Internet should revolve around the regulation of *intermediated information* or *content* exchanges. If this approach is taken, it is necessary to develop a working definition of the terms "information" and "intermediary" in this context. While these are each broad concepts, considering them in the context of existing cyberlaw cases and problems does suggest some commonalities as to how they might be defined for cyberlaw.

---

[16] Lessig, *What Cyberlaw Might Teach*, *supra* note 1.

[17] Danielle Keats Citron, *Law's Expressive Value in Combating Cyber Gender Harassment*, 108 MICH. L. REV. 373, 404 (2009) (discussing the "expressive role" law could play in the area of cyber gender harassment).

[18] *Google Spain v Costeja González*, Case C-131/12, Court of Justice for the European Union (May 13, 2014).

Most dictionary definitions contemplate that the term "information" is best defined in terms of "knowledge", "data", "communication" or "input". Most definitions comprise aspects of both content per se, and of communication of content. In other words, definitions tend to have a static aspect and an active/exchange aspect. The idea of information itself seems to comprise the importance of not simply compiling, learning or knowing something, but also the act of sharing or disseminating it with others. This is important for cyberlaw as it is the exchange component of information online that comes under the most regulatory scrutiny. While the development of new information is undoubtedly important, particularly in fields such as intellectual property, the dissemination of that information online is what comprises the basis of most Internet conflicts ranging from defamation and privacy incursions to intellectual property infringement.

In terms of digital technology, information also comes in more than one form. Notably, digital information can be input and output in human-readable forms, such as traditional human language. It can also be input and output in machine-readable forms, like binary code. Some information utilized online can be a combination of human-readable and machine-readable, meta-tags being an obvious example. Meta-tags can be used on a website to guide search engines to relevant content. They are input by individuals in traditional language, and converted to machine-readable code for search engines to index. Of course, search engines can also "read" digital text and images that form website content more generally, so in a sense all digital information comes in both a human-readable and machine-readable form. Even Internet domain names are effectively only alpha-numeric (human-readable) versions of underlying numerical IP addresses.

This book will focus on information as digital content in human readable form – including text, images, digital music and multi-media files. However, it is important to understand that at some level all of this information can be broken down into machine-readable code. Some regulatory questions confronted in cyberlaw relate to the relationship between regulating human-readable content and underlying code. In the copyright area in particular, the significance of copies of software code continually running in multiple machines to effect digital communications has been problematic in practice.

1.3.2 Intermediary

As noted above, a significant distinguishing feature of the Internet is the fact that some form of intermediary is always involved in online interactions. It is impossible for individuals to interact online without the assistance of one or more intermediaries. For instance, in the real world I can talk to my friends face to face. But in the online world, I need to employ the services of usually multiple online service provider intermediaries to communicate with others.

The definition of intermediary is challenging, but necessary to create a conception of cyberlaw that is unified and cohesive. It is the role of intermediaries that has become the central focus of much online conduct since the inception of the Internet. Intermediaries are the most effective targets for injunctions to prevent undesirable online conduct. They are also often in the best position to monitor and control communications shared over their services. The question of balancing their liabilities, and costs of such monitoring and control, against the innovative services they provide has become a central theme in all fields of Internet law including domain name regulation, intellectual property infringement, defamation, fraud, and privacy incursions.

Additionally, it is generally easier for the individual complaining about harmful online conduct to locate and serve process on an intermediary than a defendant who may be more obviously complicit in the plaintiff's harm but who may be operating anonymously/pseudonymously and may be difficult to locate geographically. Asserting personal jurisdiction over such a defendant may also be problematic, depending on where the defendant is located. Many individual defendants are also impecunious and cannot furnish a complainant with monetary damages, in cases where such a remedy is appropriate. Even where the complainant seeks injunctive relief, the cooperation of the intermediary that facilitated the harmful communications will most likely be required. For example, an intermediary can be called upon to terminate a defendant's user account or to monitor the defendant's future activities online. An injunction will also likely be more effective in practice against an intermediary that disseminates harmful information broadly even if that entity did not initially create the information in question. Again, the Google privacy decision in the Court of Justice of the European Union (CJEU) in 2014 is a good example of this dynamic. While the newspaper that wrote the story about which the defendant complained was held not to have a responsibility to delete information relating to the plaintiff, the search engine that broadly promulgated the information was liable.[19]

---

[19] *Id.*, at paras. 16–17 (noting that in the prior procedural history of the case, the newspaper that initially published the information in question was legally justified in publishing it, but that did not necessarily mean that Google was legally justified in reproducing the information in search engine results).

In the modern world, there are many different kinds of online intermediaries, a number of which will be used for case studies in this book. There are search engines, content-sharing services, payments services, retail outlets, and web-hosting services/domain name registries. All of these intermediaries enable the Internet communications that many of us take for granted. The one thing that unifies them is that they are all gateways to online communications in some way or another. They are the backbone of a system that enables the rest of us to engage in meaningful online interactions. They are also arguably the entities that most risk legal liability for the wrongful conduct of others for reasons explained in the previous section – they are the obvious choke points to monitor and control wrongful online conduct.

This book conceptualizes online intermediaries as any entity that creates a platform to enable online communications. It is undoubtedly a very broad definition and is informed by case law and legislation that has grouped these entities together when regulating online conduct. Thus, intermediaries include traditional Internet service providers such as America Online (AOL) and Yahoo! The notion of an "intermediary" also includes search engines such as Google and Bing – those entities that enable us to find information online. Electronic commerce websites such as Amazon.com and iTunes are also examples of intermediaries – those entities that enable transactions in digital information.

Online social networking platforms such as Facebook, YouTube, Pinterest and Twitter are important examples of online intermediaries that may be implicated in the wrongful conduct of their users. Individuals utilizing these services may engage in a number of different kinds of online wrongs such as bullying, harassment and copyright infringement. Because these services, unlike, say, search engines, require users to register accounts with them, they are able to employ contracts – Terms of Service agreements – to minimize their legal liability and to express their views about appropriate online conduct. Many of these services, for example, utilize detailed privacy policies.

It is important to note that the ability to utilize contracts is inherently limited to services that are in a position to require users to enter into contracts to accept their services. Some intermediaries – such as search engines – typically do not work on a "member sign-up" model, so do not utilize contracts in this way. Other intermediaries require sign-up for posting information, but, once posted, the information is generally available to the public. YouTube is an example of this model. Thus, YouTube is able to enter into contractual agreements with those who post content with it, but not with those who access content. The role of contracts in managing the liability of online intermediaries is discussed in more detail later in this book. Electronic payments systems – such as PayPal, Visa and Mastercard – are arguably also part of the intermediary framework for supporting the commercial aspects of online transactions.

Because of the central role played by intermediaries in enabling all online conduct, a cyberlaw field needs to focus significantly on appropriate approaches to regulating the conduct of those intermediaries. A strategy that places significant burdens of potential liability on these intermediaries runs the risk of chilling online innovation and communication generally, while an approach that avoids imposing any duties on intermediaries runs the risk of inadvertently condoning wrongful online conduct. The ill-fated Stop Online Piracy Act (SOPA) was perhaps an example of the former approach, while the implementation of § 230 of the Communications Decency Act (CDA) in the United States is arguably an example of the latter.

A reconceptualized cyberlaw field could serve to organize the judicial and legislative developments from disparate areas of law that relate to intermediaries into a more cohesive framework. Currently, online service providers within the United States face completely different approaches to liability in fields such as copyright, trademark and defamation law. Even within those fields, questions of primary versus secondary liability for online service providers remain largely unanswered. There is no uniform approach as to when and whether an intermediary should be sued in primary versus secondary liability in fields such as copyright or trademark law. The picture is even more confusing for such service providers across national borders.

The remainder of this book comprises detailed examination, drawing heavily from existing case law and legislation, of the central role played by online intermediaries in Internet-based transactions. It attempts to draw common threads between intermediary issues that have arisen across distinct legal fields. Focusing on recent developments in the digital content marketplace, along with case law and legislation from the United States and other jurisdictions involving online conduct, the author attempts to create a more cohesive approach to cyberlaw going forward. Many of the case studies revolve around attempts to balance interests in intellectual property and privacy against free speech and other public interests in the online context. These questions go to the heart of Internet regulation because cyberlaw is all about content regulation and the balance between access to, and control of, digital information. The key point is that because intermediaries are essential to all online conduct they are in a unique position as a focal point of Internet regulation.

The following chapters focus respectively on the role of intermediaries in online information exchanges in the context of digital copyright law, trademark and Internet domain name law, defamation and associated tort law, and privacy law. The final chapter draws together the threads of the discussions involving specific areas of law and suggestions future directions for cyberlaw development.

1.4 CHAPTER SUMMARY: THE CONTOURS OF CYBERLAW

While no book can answer every possible question about future directions for the development of the cyberlaw field, the aim of this book is to reconceptualize the basic tenets of the field so debates about future regulation of the Internet can be more cohesive and pragmatic. In particular, it is important to move the debate away from questions about *whether* cyberlaw is a distinct field toward what the field actually comprises. The subject has endured in law school curricula and does have something important to contribute to law reform efforts provided that it is conceptualized in a more unified manner with a focus on intermediated information exchange. The central tenets of the field are therefore: information and intermediaries.

Related themes include jurisdictional questions, the relationship between legal rules and other regulatory modalities, the role of law as a regulatory force online (as compared with other modalities of regulation), and appropriate remedies for online harm. It is obvious from this description that the discussions in this book will consciously focus on "law" as regulator of online conduct, as contrasted with these other modalities. While it is not possible to consider law in a vacuum, much existing cyberlaw literature has argued that law becomes less relevant in the digital age and other forces may be more effective as regulators.[20]

It is important to focus back on the appropriate role for legal regulation online, rather than making the assumption that law should take a back seat to system architecture and social norms. While it may be true that law is less important online as a regulator than in the physical world, the law does have something to contribute to Internet regulation, and it would be inadvisable to overlook its importance.

---

[20] See, for example, notes 1 and 3, *supra*, and accompanying text.

2. Digital copyright law

2.1 COPYRIGHT IN CYBERSPACE

2.1.1 The Digital Challenge for Copyright Law

A logical place to commence a reconsideration of cyberlaw is with the myriad challenges posed by digital technology to copyright law. These were some of the earliest legal issues identified in online regulation and a number of them still remain unresolved. Copyright law is particularly problematic in cyberspace because it is premised on control of protected "works", many of which are information products, including literary works, computer software, and digital versions of music and movies. Because the nature of digital technology revolves around machines making copies of software code, text, graphics and the like, the Internet is replete with copies of works that are technically unauthorized but many of which are functionally necessary for the effective operation of the network. Along with this incidental copying that is necessary for network operations is the ease with which pirates and others can copy and distribute protected works globally at the press of a button in ways that may or may not interfere with the commercial profit margins of copyright holders depending on the context.

The other distinguishing feature of digital technology in respect of unauthorized copying, at least in contrast to previous modes of copying, is that digital copies are perfect or near perfect and can compete effectively with original works in the online world:

> Digital technology and the exponential growth of the Internet threaten to upset copyright law's delicate balance. Once converted to digital files, many works of authorship, including text, music, graphics, and video can be flawlessly copied at almost no cost. Subsequent copies can be made with no degradation in the quality of these copies as happens in the analog world. Once in digital form, these same files can then be distributed globally using

> the Internet at virtually no cost. Technology, therefore, makes it possible for anyone with a computer to become a global distributor of copyrighted works.[1]

Of course, digital technology also enables copyright holders to protect their copyrights on a scope and scale never before possible. Through the use of copyright management information, copyright holders are able to assert individual terms of use and ownership information in relation to protected works.[2] More importantly, digital technology can be utilized to control what downstream users can do with individual copies of works. For example, technological measures can be utilized to prevent access to or copying of a work, allow a user to access a work only a specified number of times or only after paying a fee, delete a copy of a work after a certain date, automatically bill for access to a work, etc.

---

[1] RAYMOND KU and JACQUELINE LIPTON, CYBERSPACE LAW: CASES AND MATERIALS, 356 (3 ed, 2010).

[2] "Copyright management information" is defined in 17 U.S.C. § 1202(c) as "As used in this section, the term 'copyright management information' means any of the following information conveyed in connection with copies or phonorecords of a work or performances or displays of a work, including in digital form, except that such term does not include any personally identifying information about a user of a work or of a copy, phonorecord, performance, or display of a work:

> (1) The title and other information identifying the work, including the information set forth on a notice of copyright.
> (2) The name of, and other identifying information about, the author of a work.
> (3) The name of, and other identifying information about, the copyright owner of the work, including the information set forth in a notice of copyright.
> (4) With the exception of public performances of works by radio and television broadcast stations, the name of, and other identifying information about, a performer whose performance is fixed in a work other than an audiovisual work.
> (5) With the exception of public performances of works by radio and television broadcast stations, in the case of an audiovisual work, the name of, and other identifying information about, a writer, performer, or director who is credited in the audiovisual work.
> (6) Terms and conditions for use of the work.
> (7) Identifying numbers or symbols referring to such information or links to such information.
> (8) Such other information as the Register of Copyrights may prescribe by regulation, except that the Register of Copyrights may not require the provision of any information concerning the user of a copyrighted work."

An examination of online copyright questions also supports the characterization of the central tenets of cyberlaw set out in Chapter 1 as revolving around information and online intermediaries. To illustrate this point, subsequent chapters of this book compare digital copyright regulation with regulatory paradigms developed in other fields including trademark infringement, defamation, privacy incursions, and online bullying and harassment. The comparison of copyright law to these other fields enables us to draw together common threads of cyberspace law that have been missed or glossed over in past discussions. In other words, the suggested focus on the role of online intermediaries in regulating information exchanges in these various fields of law will illuminate the cyberlaw field more generally and will provide useful directions for future organization of the field that are more cohesive than current approaches.

2.1.2 Emerging Themes in Digital Copyright Regulation

Some of the themes for copyright law that have emerged since the early days of the Internet resonate powerfully with the central tenets of this book. Most major copyright litigation, and new digital copyright legislative initiatives, have revolved around issues of Internet intermediary liability for copyright infringement. Direct copyright infringers can be difficult to locate in practice and may be impecunious or outside the plaintiff's jurisdiction, making litigation against them costly and potentially ineffective.

Focusing on intermediaries – those who enable the activities of the direct infringers – avoids many of these difficulties. Intermediaries are easier for plaintiffs to locate. They are effective targets for injunctions. They are potentially easier to negotiate with than direct infringers as it is usually in their best interests to stamp out illegal activities that utilize their services. Thus, intermediaries have become the focus of most digital copyright law. Online services as varied as the Google and Netscape search engines, smaller bulletin board operators, online file-sharing services, as well as online retailers and social networks have all been subjects of copyright litigation.

However, the focus on these entities necessitates resolution of a number of questions that form the basis for the discussions in this chapter. In particular, the need to determine the role of intermediaries in copyright infringement requires consideration of the following:

(a) As many intermediaries' underlying software makes copies of protected works, even where the intermediary itself has not instigated the infringement, the question arises as to the extent to which such intermediaries should be potentially held *primarily* versus *secondarily* liable for copyright infringement. While primary infringement is a strict liability tort,[3] some secondary liability requires a *mens rea* component on the part of the infringer,[4] or, in the case of vicarious liability, requires that the intermediary have the ability to monitor and control the direct infringer's conduct.[5] This is a potentially significant fact for a plaintiff in establishing a case of infringement, particularly in situations where the intermediary did not have the requisite state of mind or ability to monitor the defendant's activities.

(b) Where secondary liability is the focus of the action, the determination of the appropriate level of knowledge or participation by the intermediary in the primary infringer's conduct can be difficult to ascertain in the context of largely automated copying.

(c) In both the primary and secondary infringement contexts, the interpretation of copyright terms of art has proved challenging. Some of the specific issues addressed in the case law have included the nature of a "copy" online,[6] and the application of concepts such as display or performance of works to the public online.[7] In recent years the notion of a "public" display or performance has proved highly problematic for copyright law in the digital context.[8] These definitional questions based, as they are, on the wording of the copyright statute, are specific to copyright law. However, the

---

[3] JOHN TEHRANIAN, INFRINGEMENT NATION, 146 (2011) (noting strict liability basis of copyright law).

[4] PATRY ON COPYRIGHT, § 21:41 ("the essence of contributory infringement is knowledge of the infringing conduct and facilitating the means by which the direct infringement is accomplished").

[5] *Id.* ("The essence of vicarious liability is the right to control the infringing conduct and derivation of a financial benefit from that conduct").

[6] The statutory definition of "copy" is found in 17 U.S.C. § 101, and is discussed in more detail *infra*.

[7] The statutory definition of "display" is found in 17 U.S.C. § 101, and is discussed in more detail *infra*.

[8] See, for example, discussion of recent cases in: Jacqueline Lipton, *Digital Video Streaming in the United States Supreme Court: American Broadcasting Commission v Aereo*, 88 AUSTRALIAN LAW JOURNAL 302 (2014) [hereinafter, *Digital Video Streaming*]; *American Broadcasting Corporation v Aereo*, 573 U.S. ___ (2014).

necessity for courts to review familiar concepts in new contexts is especially germane to cyberlaw, and the new contexts often raise similar issues of interpretation, particularly where results will impact the cost and effectiveness of innovations in online services.

(d) Defenses to infringement are a common theme in copyright cases, notably the application of the fair use defense.[9] Again, the application of copyright defenses are specific to copyright law. However, they are of general interest in a broader discussion of the contours of cyberlaw because the application of defenses in all fields of law online involve a delicate balance between protecting existing legal interests against the needs for Internet users to be able to communicate freely online. Some other fields of law, such as trademark law, also utilize "fair use" concepts, but they operate differently, as discussed in more detail in the following chapter.

(e) The need for specific new legislation to deal with digital challenges. In the copyright context, a comprehensive legislative package – the Digital Millennium Copyright Act – was enacted in the United States in 1998. Many other jurisdictions took similar approaches.[10] The main focus of the laws was on dealing with some of the issues identified earlier in this chapter: for example, ascertaining the appropriate scope of legal liability for online intermediaries, and regulating the use of digital technologies to protect works against unauthorized access and use. The need for specific new legislative initiatives is another common theme in cyberlaw regulation and has arisen in a number of fields throughout multiple jurisdictions.

(f) The extent to which existing legal paradigms make sense in the digital age, or whether new legal paradigms are necessary in cyberspace. While this question has been raised in relation to copyright law,[11] it is another theme that permeates the study of cyberlaw more generally.

---

[9] 17 U.S.C. § 107.

[10] See, for example, Copyright, Designs and Patents Act (1988), Eng., Part VII.

[11] MARSHALL LEAFFER, UNDERSTANDING COPYRIGHT LAW, 25 (5 ed, 2010) ("As copyright and the world move into the Third Millennium, a development in information technology, which may have as much potential for social transformation as did movable type, is leading some to question the continued relevance of traditional copyright law").

Before considering any of these questions in detail, however, it is necessary to have a basic understanding of what copyright law is and how it worked prior to the Internet age.

2.2 COPYRIGHT LAW BASICS

2.2.1 Copyrighted Works

Copyright law deals with a very particular kind of information product that defies traditional real property paradigms. While information products such as movies, books and music can be costly to create, they do not raise the problems of scarcity inherent in physical property. In other words, while there is only so much workable farmland available in the real world, an information product can be enjoyed by infinite numbers of people without diminishing the *amount* of the information. As noted by Professor Leaffer: "If someone steals my automobile, I am deprived of it. My automobile is finite and exhaustible, whereas my song is infinite and inexhaustible".[12] This characteristic of information products is often referred to as "non-rivalrousness" or, in economic theory, as the fact that information products are "public goods".[13] Non-rivalrousness may be explained by saying that the ownership of a copy of a work (song, movie, book) by one person does not prevent another from simultaneously enjoying her own copy of the same work. A public good is a good that is "inappropriable" in the sense that it can never truly be "appropriated" from the original owner/creator in the physical sense. Its value may be diminished if multiple people enjoy the work without compensation to the creator. But the work itself cannot be physically appropriated.[14]

The notion of a "work" is at the heart of copyright law. Copyright protects individual works of authorship against the infringement of exclusive rights granted to the author by statute. In the United States, § 102(a) of Title 17 of the United States Code (the copyright act) provides that:

> Copyright protection subsists, in accordance with this title, in original works of authorship fixed in any tangible medium of expression, now known or later developed, from which they can be perceived, reproduced, or otherwise

---

[12] *Id.*, at 22.
[13] *Id.*, at 23.
[14] *Id.*

communicated, either directly or with the aid of a machine or device. Works of authorship include the following categories:

(1) literary works;
(2) musical works, including any accompanying words;
(3) dramatic works, including any accompanying music;
(4) pantomimes and choreographic works;
(5) pictorial, graphic, and sculptural works;
(6) motion pictures and other audiovisual works;
(7) sound recordings; and
(8) architectural works.

Copyright law was initially enacted to protect literary texts in the wake of the development of the printing press.[15] However, modern copyright law clearly covers a much broader array of original works of authorship, most of which can be produced and disseminated in digital form including movies, music, computer software and video games. While computer software and video games are not expressly mentioned in § 102(a), they are protected variously as compilations, audiovisual works, literary works, movies and graphical works.[16] In some countries, these works are protected expressly in copyright legislation.[17]

2.2.2 Exclusive Rights of the Copyright Holder

The exclusive rights reserved to a copyright holder are enumerated in § 106 of the copyright act. Section 106 provides that:

[T]he owner of copyright … has the exclusive rights to do and to authorize any of the following:

(1) to reproduce the copyrighted work in copies or phonorecords;
(2) to prepare derivative works based upon the copyrighted work;

---

[15] *Id.*, at 25 ("Just as the printing press gave rise to the need for copyright law, new technologies have created the further need for legislative response").

[16] See, for example, discussion in PATRY ON COPYRIGHT, at § 3.81 (on video games); Jacqueline Lipton, *IP's Problem Child: Shifting the Paradigms for Software Protection*, 58 HASTINGS LAW JOURNAL 205 (2006) (on computer software generally).

[17] See, for example; Copyright, Designs and Patents Act (1988), Eng., §§ 1(b) and (d) protecting computer software and databases respectively as "literary works".

(3) to distribute copies or phonorecords of the copyrighted work to the public by sale or other transfer of ownership, or by rental, lease, or lending;
(4) in the case of literary, musical, dramatic, and choreographic works, pantomimes, and motion pictures and other audiovisual works, to perform the copyrighted work publicly;
(5) in the case of literary, musical, dramatic, and choreographic works, pantomimes, and pictorial, graphic, or sculptural works, including the individual images of a motion picture or other audiovisual work, to display the copyrighted work publicly; and
(6) in the case of sound recordings, to perform the copyrighted work publicly by means of a digital audio transmission.

The boundaries of some of these rights will be considered in the following discussion as they are applied to activities of online intermediaries. It is important to bear in mind that the exclusive rights inhere in the copyright holder who may or may not be the original author, artist or creator of the work. As a property right (or at least a property-like right), copyright is assignable from its original creator to others. Often authors and artists will assign their copyrights to publishers, producers and distributors of commercially valuable works. Generally, copyright inheres in the author at the time of a work's creation, but is often transferred to another entity subsequently, usually in order to be commercialized. Some countries also allow "works for hire" where a creator is contracted by a producer to create works that will, on creation, legally belong to the producer.[18]

Inherent in this discussion of ownership of copyrights is the underlying interest in commercialization of valuable information products. One of the key challenges to copyright law in the digital age has revolved around concerns about the ease with which unauthorized copying and dissemination of valuable works will ultimately disincentivize creation. As noted by Professor Leaffer: "Without the ability to exclude others in the networked environment, information providers will have little incentive to disseminate works that take a heavy investment in time and effort. The fear is that we may be left with these wonderful digital copying and transmission technologies with less and less worth copying".[19]

---

[18] See, for example, 17 U.S.C. § 201(b) ("In the case of a work made for hire, the employer or other person for whom the work was prepared is considered the author for purposes of this title, and, unless the parties have expressly agreed otherwise in a written instrument signed by them, owns all of the rights comprised in the copyright").

[19] LEAFFER, *supra* note 11, at 28.

2.2.3 The Idea/Expression Dichotomy

The American copyright legislation articulates the distinction in § 102(b): "In no case does copyright protection for an original work of authorship extend to any idea, procedure, process, system, method of operation, concept, principle, or discovery, regardless of the form in which it is described, explained, illustrated, or embodied in such work". The point of the distinction is to facilitate creative expression in society generally, an underlying policy basis of copyright law. As expressed by Professor Leaffer, "To create new works, future authors must have access to a well-endowed public domain, the place where fundamental building materials – concepts, discoveries and technological solutions – reside and are freely available for those wishing to embellish them with their own original expression".[20] In the United States, the idea of allowing others to use ideas once injected into the public domain is also consistent with the First Amendment. A more restrictive copyright law would potentially impinge on the free exchange of information and ideas. Of course the boundaries of the idea–expression distinction are not necessarily clear-cut in practice. American copyright law protects against unauthorized exploitation of a work that is "substantially similar" to the copyright holder's work,[21] allowing at least some leeway to protect aspects of the underlying idea.

2.3 COPYRIGHT AND THE LAW OF THE GLOBAL INTERMEDIATED INFORMATION EXCHANGE

2.3.1 Protecting Copyright Versus Promoting Technological Innovation

The development of copyright law in cyberspace is a paradigm example of the issues identified in the previous chapter as the central tenets of cyberlaw – the fact that cyberlaw regulates *intermediated information exchanges*. As an information product, copyrighted works lie at the heart of online regulation. They raise the specter of balancing the free exchange of information and ideas on a global scale with the need to protect proprietary interests in intangible property. As with all online conduct, all information exchanges involving copyrighted material will

[20] *Id.*, at 78–79.
[21] *Id.*, at 79.

implicate at least one, if not more, online intermediaries including search engines, online retailers, social networks, and even electronic payments systems.

As noted by the Supreme Court in the *Grokster* litigation, involving unauthorized peer-to-peer file-sharing of digital music, much of modern digital copyright litigation is about the delicate balance between "the respective values of supporting creative pursuits through copyright protection and promoting innovation in new communication technologies by limiting the incidence of liability for copyright infringement".[22] Inevitably, as the Court pointed out, "The more artistic protection is favored, the more technological innovation may be discouraged; the administration of copyright law is an exercise in managing the trade-off ...".[23]

The Supreme Court's approach sums up not only the nature of digital copyright law, but also of cyberlaw more generally. The more rigorously existing legal rights are protected (including intellectual property rights, rights to privacy and protection of one's reputation), the more burdens are potentially thrust upon those providing innovative digital communications services. The more burdens are thrust upon digital service providers, the greater the threat of chilling innovations in digital technology, or at least making them expensive or unwieldy to operate. Internet intermediaries are implicated at the crossroads of the balance because they are the ones most likely to become caught up in litigation, or be the subject of new legislative initiatives to protect legal rights.

2.3.2 Direct Infringement

Some of the earliest questions to be considered by American courts involving digital copyright issues included the extent to which early intermediaries – such as basic Internet service providers and bulletin board operators – could potentially be held directly or primarily liable for copyright infringement in situations where they had not initiated the postings of infringing material.

The resolution of the question of direct liability for copyright infringement in these circumstances has required a close analysis of the wording of the copyright act with respect to definitions of terms like "copies". In order to be a direct copyright infringer, the defendant is not required to

---

[22] *MGM v Grokster*, 545 U.S. 913, 928 (2005).

[23] *Id.* More recently, the Supreme Court made similar comments in *American Broadcasting Corporation v Aereo*, 573 U.S. ___ (2014) (noting the importance of applying copyright law so as not to "discourage or to control the emergence or use of different kinds of technologies").

have any particular *mens rea* or intention to infringe copyright. Direct infringement is a matter of strict liability.[24] However, the defendant does have to have infringed one of the exclusive rights reserved to the copyright holder. The key rights generally implicated in digital copyright cases have revolved around the rights of reproduction, public performance, public display, distribution, and in some cases the creation of derivative works.[25] In terms of the reproduction right, and according to some judges also the distribution and display rights,[26] the defendant has to have made or disseminated *copies* of a protected work as defined in the legislation.

The definition of "copies" in the American legislation requires a material object in which a work is fixed and from which it can be perceived, reproduced or otherwise communicated.[27] A work is "fixed" in a tangible medium of expression for copyright purposes when "its embodiment in a copy or phonorecord … is sufficiently permanent or stable to permit it to be perceived, reproduced, or otherwise communicated for a period of more than transitory duration".[28]

While these definitional questions appear at first glance to be largely technical issues, they are extremely important in ascertaining whether the activities of online intermediaries result in copies that are sufficiently "fixed" for the purposes of the legislation. Copies of works that are stored on intermediaries' servers as a result of being uploaded by another person may be temporary: for example, where they are buffered or cached in the intermediaries' systems. Questions of fixation were central to the courts in two leading digital age decisions – *MAI Systems v Peak Computer*[29] and *Cartoon Network v Cablevision*.[30]

Neither of these cases was a typical "Internet intermediary" case in the sense that the defendants were not online service providers. Each provided a service to customers but neither did so over the Internet. In *MAI*, the defendant was a computer servicing company that ran copies of copyrighted software in order to diagnose problems with the machines, and in *Cartoon Network*, the defendant was a cable service provider that recorded home television programs at the request of its customers.

However, both are seminal cases on the interpretation of "fixation" for the purposes of defining "copies" under the United States copyright act.

---

24 TEHRANIAN, *supra* note 3.

25 17 U.S.C. § 106.

26 See, for example, *Playboy v Frena*, 839 F. Supp. 1552 (M.D. Fla. 1993).

27 17 U.S.C. § 101.

28 *Id.*

29 991 F.2d 511 (9th Cir. 1993).

30 536 F.3d 121 (2008).

While the *MAI* court held that running a copy of a protected program in the Random Access Memory (RAM) of a computer was sufficient fixation for a copy to be made under the legislation,[31] the court in *Cartoon Network* held that storing portions of television programs for small amounts of time while buffering them in its system was not sufficient fixation for copyright purposes. The works were not stored "for a period of more than transitory duration" as required by the definition of "fixed".[32]

Early digital copyright cases revolved around questions whether a bulletin board operator or Internet service provider might be directly or secondarily liable for information stored on its servers or cached that had been initially posted by a customer infringing a copyright holder's exclusive rights.[33] While some courts held that the intermediaries should be held liable for maintaining copies of the infringing works despite their lack of intention to infringe copyrights or more active participation in copyright infringement,[34] others however demurred for various reasons.

In *Religious Technology Center v Netcom*, the District Court of the Northern District of California held that Internet intermediaries were not directly liable for infringements where their customers had originated the postings of the infringing material. The court accepted that direct infringement "does not require intent or any particular state of mind".[35] Nevertheless, Judge White noted that where the copying by the intermediary is a purely technical process in which the defendant has not taken any affirmative action other than installing and maintaining a system under which software automatically copies messages from others on to its servers, the defendant cannot be said to have "caused" the copying.[36] This same reasoning was taken up in a second part of the *Cartoon Networks* case involving the storing and replaying of full copies of copyrighted television programs at the request of Cablevision's customers as distinct from the part of the decision that focused on

---

31 See *supra* note 29.

32 *Cartoon Network v Cablevision*, 536 F.3d. 121, 129–30 (2008).

33 *Playboy Enterprises v Frena*, *supra* note 26; *Religious Technology Center v Netcom*, 907 F. Supp. 1361 (N.D. Cal. 1995).

34 *Frena*, *supra* note 46, at 1559 ("There is irrefutable evidence of direct copyright infringement in this case. It does not matter that Defendant Frena may have been unaware of the copyright infringement. Intent to infringe is not needed to find copyright infringement. Intent or knowledge is not an element of the infringement, and thus even an innocent infringer is liable for infringement …").

35 *Religious Technology Center*, *supra* note 33, at 1367.

36 *Id.*, at 1368.

transitory buffered copies. Employing a variation of the "volition" argument accepted by the court in *Netcom*, the *Cartoon Networks* court held that it was the customer, rather than Cablevision, that caused the full copies to be made and that Cablevision was providing a purely mechanical process, much like a set-top digital video recorder.[37]

In cases where the defendant–intermediary's activities have not been sufficient to establish primary infringement, the defendant may nevertheless potentially be secondarily liable for infringements where infringing postings have been initiated by others. Secondary infringement is examined in more detail in Part 2.3.4 below. However, it is perhaps worth noting here for completeness that the defendant in *Cartoon Network* could not have been held secondary liable for copyright infringement because American copyright law exempts as fair use the home-recording of television programs for later viewing.[38] If Cablevision itself was not a primary infringer, it could not have been held secondarily liable for primary infringements conducted by its individual customers because those customers could avail themselves of the fair use defense to copyright infringement and would not be liable as primary infringers. With no primary infringers, there would be no primary conduct for which Cablevision could be held secondarily liable.

Other variations on the primary liability question for Internet intermediaries have also arisen outside the bulletin board and Internet service provider context. In two well-known cases in the United States, courts have been faced with questions about the extent to which Internet search engines might be held liable for copyright infringements with respect to their search results. The two leading American cases have involved copyrighted images which are typically reproduced in search engine results in several ways. Search engines such as Google make thumbnail versions of digital images that are displayed in image search results. Additionally, they inline link to full-scale versions of the pictures on the original websites. While the thumbnail images involve the search engine actually making a low resolution version of the image and displaying it, the inline linking is technically a frame to the original page on which the image appears. The search engine does not actually copy the full-scale image as a mechanical process, even though the Internet user has no way of knowing the difference. The respective courts in *Kelly v ArribaSoft*[39]

---

37 *Cartoon Network*, *supra* note 32.

38 *Sony v University City Studios*, 464 U.S. 417 (1984).

39 336 F.3d 811 (2003).

and *Perfect 10 v Google*[40] each held that while the reproduction of an image as a thumbnail copy could amount to a direct copyright infringement, subject to the fair use defense, the inline linking did not involve a "copy" and could not be a direct infringement on the part of the search engines.

Distinct questions about statutory interpretation of the copyright act in the context of the public performance right have recently arisen involving intermediaries who display copies of video content at the behest of customers who are otherwise legally entitled to receive them.[41] Both *Cablevision*, and the case of *American Broadcasting Commission v Aereo*,[42] considered whether an intermediary could have infringed the public performance right by displaying individual copies of copyrighted programs to individual customers on request. Both the *Cablevision* and *Aereo* systems were set up to create individual copies of programs for individual customers, necessitating wasteful duplication of resources. While the *Cablevision* court held that where an individual copy is received by an individual customer, there is no "public performance" in infringement of § 106,[43] the Supreme Court in *Aereo* disagreed. The Supreme Court held that it was immaterial that individual copies were received by individual customers. If the performance was available to a broad group of the public, it was a public performance.[44]

This question of statutory interpretation under the copyright act is another example of ways in which disruptive new technologies challenge existing interpretations of terms in the copyright statute. Any determination a court makes will involve prioritizing either an intermediary over a copyright holder or vice versa. In *Cablevision*, the court held that there was no infringement of the public performance right when the defendant stored and displayed individual copies of programs to its customers.

This question involving the interpretation of the public performance right brings into sharp relief the problems when laws as currently drafted

---

40 487 F.3d 701 (9th Cir 2007).

41 17 U.S.C. § 106(4).

42 573 U.S. ___ (2014).

43 *Cartoon Network*, *supra* note 32, at 139 ("[W]e find that the transmit clause directs us to identify the potential audience of a given transmission, i.e., the persons 'capable of receiving' it, to determine whether that transmission is made 'to the public.' Because each RS–DVR playback transmission is made to a single subscriber using a single unique copy produced by that subscriber, we conclude that such transmissions are not performances 'to the public,' and therefore do not infringe any exclusive right of public performance").

44 *Aereo*, *supra* note 42.

require a binary decision where either technological innovation wins or copyright holders win. An ability to reconsider the notion of public performance more generally, with a view to both protecting copyrights and encouraging non-wasteful innovations in digital distribution technologies, would be useful. A reconceived cyberlaw framework focusing on these kinds of issues could assist in the development of such approaches. Ultimately, the answers may require redrafting of legislation in some cases.

2.3.3 Internet Service Provider Safe Harbor Legislation

In order to protect online service providers from claims of digital copyright liability, the legislatures in many countries implemented "safe harbor" statutes for online service providers. In drafting safe harbor provisions, legislators were naturally faced with difficult questions of the extent to which such entities should be required or at least encouraged to monitor and control the activities of those who utilized their services. In the United States, Congress enacted the Online Copyright Infringement Liability Limitations Act (OCILLA) as part of the Digital Millennium Copyright Act in 1998. The OCILLA inserted a new § 512 into the copyright act to deal with questions of online service provider liability for copyright infringements initiated by others. These provisions work alongside the common law of secondary liability and, in practice, tend to operate as a defense to claims of secondary copyright liability. The application of secondary theories of copyright infringement to online service providers is considered in the following section.

The American legislation creates four separate "safe harbors" for service providers engaging in particular activities: transitory network communications;[45] storage;[46] caching;[47] and, providing links via information search tools (search engines).[48] Unsurprisingly, considering the pre-existing case-law, the legislative provision most often cited in litigation, and the one with the most practical impact, is that dealing with information stored on a service provider's system or network that has been uploaded by another person: 17 U.S.C. § 512(c). It covers situations where an entity providing an online service has little to no control and little ability to effectively monitor material posted by others.

This sub-section provides that:

45 17 U.S.C. § 512(a).
46 17 U.S.C. § 512(c).
47 17 U.S.C. § 512(b).
48 17 U.S.C. § 512(d).

> A service provider shall not be liable … for infringement of copyright by reason of the storage *at the direction of a user* of material that resides on a system or network controlled or operated by or for the service provider, if the service provider –
>
> (A) (i) does not have actual knowledge that the material or an activity using the material on the system or network is infringing;
> (ii) in the absence of such actual knowledge, is not aware of facts or circumstances from which infringing activity is apparent; or
> (iii) upon obtaining such knowledge or awareness, acts expeditiously to remove, or disable access to, the material;
>
> (B) does not receive a financial benefit directly attributable to the infringing activity, in a case in which the service provider has the right and ability to control such activity; and
>
> (C) upon notification of claimed infringement … responds expeditiously to remove, or disable access to, the material that is claimed to be infringing or to be the subject of infringing activity. (*emphasis added)*

For the purposes of this sub-section, "service provider" is defined as an entity that provides online services or network access, or operates the facilities therefor, and includes an entity that offers transmission, routing or providing of connections for digital online communications without modifying the content of the material sent or received.[49] This definition is obviously broad enough to encompass entities such as basic Internet access providers as well as bulletin board operators. However, it will also include social networking services such as Facebook, video-sharing services such as YouTube and even Internet search engines, as specifically contemplated in the safe harbor for search engines found in 17 U.S.C. § 512(d).

For completeness, it is worth noting that the definition of "service provider" for the purposes of the safe harbor dealing with transitory communications – 17 U.S.C. § 512(a) – is limited to: "an entity offering the transmission, routing, or providing of connections for digital online communications, between or amongst points specified by a user, of material of the user's choosing, without modification to the content of the material as sent or received". This is because the wording of the safe harbor for transitory data communications is not predicated on any form of knowledge on the part of the service provider in question. The provision can work more simply if limited to those who, at no point, store or monitor content that is temporarily transmitted via their networks.

---

49 17 U.S.C. § 512(k)(1).

The safe harbor for system caching also works a little differently to those for storage and search in the sense that the knowledge requirement is a little different. The caching safe harbor only applies to service providers who cache content as a purely automated technical process and who remove the material expeditiously on receiving a copyright infringement notice from a copyright holder.[50] The safe harbors for storage and for search engines each utilize a knowledge standard derived from the common law relating to contributory and vicarious copyright infringement, as is evidenced by the wording of § 512(c)(1)(A) and (B), above. With respect to search engines, this wording is mirrored in the specific search engine safe harbor provision: 17 U.S.C. § 512(d)(1) and (2).

The safe harbor for storage in § 512(c) is only available to a service provider who designates an agent to receive copyright infringement notices and makes the contact information for the agent available as specified in the legislation.[51] The sub-section also sets out requirements for an effective copyright infringement notification.[52] In so doing, this particular safe harbor creates a relatively intricate balance between the rights and obligations of the copyright holder and the online service provider in terms of protecting copyrights versus promoting technological innovation.

While it is beyond the scope of this discussion to undertake a comprehensive comparative analysis of copyright – or other laws – online, it is worth noting that copyright is one field in which countries have been relatively harmonized in their legislative approach, at least in terms of the key issues confronting copyright holders globally at the dawn of the digital age. Consequently, most other major intellectual property trading nations have implemented safe harbor legislation. The European Union, for example, included safe harbor provisions for transitory data communications, caching and information storage in its Electronic Commerce Directive in 2000.[53] These provisions have been implemented into domestic law in European Union Member States.

Safe harbor legislation for online service providers in the copyright context has been one of the success stories where legislatures have attempted to address the balance between promoting existing legal

---

[50] 17 U.S.C. § 512(b).

[51] 17 U.S.C. § 512(c)(2).

[52] 17 U.S.C. § 512(c)(3).

[53] Directive 2000/31/EC of the European Parliament and of the Council of 8 June 2000 on certain legal aspects of information society services, in particular electronic commerce, in the Internal Market ('Directive on electronic commerce'), arts. 12, 13 and 14 respectively.

interests (in this case, copyrights) while at the same time facilitating online innovation in communications technologies. There have been plenty of examples of less successful attempts to address this balance. One glaring example is the Stop Online Piracy Act (SOPA) which was proposed to impose a greater burden on online intermediaries to help prevent copyright infringement. This bill generated a significant amount of media attention as well as leading to the infamous "service blackout" by leading service providers including Wikipedia and Google. It was never enacted into law. The media frenzy and associated debates surrounding SOPA demonstrate the importance of striking the appropriate balance between existing legal rights and the promotion of innovation in online services. The fact that online service providers had sufficient clout to raise awareness in the way they did is a testament to the importance of ensuring that their interests – and those of their members/users – are protected in legislative initiatives.

2.3.4 Secondary Liability for Copyright Infringement

2.3.4.1 Contributory and vicarious liability

While online intermediaries have generally been shielded from direct liability for copyright infringement – at least in cases where they have not initiated the copying or where copies have been created through purely technical means and where they have acted expeditiously to remove infringing content on notice – the doorway has been kept open for secondary liability, subject to the safe harbor provisions discussed above. Secondary infringement in the United States revolves around issues of knowledge and participation in infringement (for the purposes of contributory infringement)[54] and direct financial benefit in circumstances where the defendant has the ability to monitor and control the infringement (for the purposes of vicarious liability).[55]

Secondary infringement is a matter of common law. Contributory liability stems from the tort law principle that a person who directly contributes to the infringement of another should be held accountable.[56] Vicarious liability in the copyright context developed initially from principles of agency law involving the idea of *respondeat superior*.[57] Each of these principles has developed in the digital age to apply to various activities of online service providers. Contributory liability, in

---

54 LEAFFER, *supra* note 11, at 438.

55 *Id.*, at 445.

56 *Id.*, at 438.

57 *Id.*, at 445.

particular, has undergone a significant judicial metamorphosis in light of the United States Supreme Court's decision in *MGM v Grokster*,[58] which is discussed in detail below.

Prior to the *Grokster* decision, it was relatively well-settled that contributory liability might arise where a defendant has knowledge of an infringing activity and induces, causes or materially contributes to the infringing conduct of another.[59] However, many of the early digital cases arose in situations where the defendant online service provider did not directly *induce* infringement, but may possibly have had actual or constructive knowledge of infringement, particularly on receipt of a complaint by a copyright-holder. The possibility of contributory infringement of an Internet service provider with respect to material posted on its servers by others was acknowledged in *Religious Technology Center v Netcom* as early as 1995.[60] When digital file-sharing services started to become popular in the late 1990s and early 2000s, courts focused on the likelihood that intermediary defendants had actual or constructive knowledge of primary infringements.

For example, in the case of *A&M Records v Napster*,[61] involving an unauthorized peer-to-peer music file-sharing service, the court rejected the defendant's argument that it did not have sufficient knowledge of the illegal file sharing conducted by its customers, particularly in the wake of complaints by the recording industry about copyright infringement.[62] Napster was not liable for direct infringement because no actual copies of protected works were made on its servers. Its software simply enabled private individuals to share music amongst themselves by providing a central indexing function directing its users to other users who had copies of requested .mp3 recordings on their own hard drives.

Hot on the heels of Napster's demise, new file-sharing services Grokster and Streamcast effectively "coded around" the *Napster* holding in creating a file sharing service with no central-indexing function to give them sufficient knowledge of customer infringements, in an attempt to avoid secondary liability. While their arguments shielding them from secondary liability were successful in the Ninth Circuit,[63] the Supreme Court overturned that decision. The Supreme Court drew on earlier

---

[58] 125 S. Ct. 2764 (2005); 545 U.S. 913 (2005).

[59] *Gershwin Publishing Corp v Columbia Artists Management*, 443 F.2d 1159, 1162 (2d Cir. 1971).

[60] See *supra* note 35.

[61] 239 F.3d 1004 (2001).

[62] *Id.*

[63] *MGM v Grokster*, 259 F. Supp.2d 1029 (2003).

common law formulations of contributory liability which contemplated a secondary defendant's "inducement" of the primary infringers' activities. On this basis, it held the defendant file-sharing services liable.[64]

The Court held that the defendants were liable for inducing the activities of their customers because they actively sought to fill the gap left in the marketplace for illegal file sharing when Napster went out of business.[65] The Court considered evidence of internal documentation of business plans to exploit this market as well as the fact that the defendants made no attempt to use screening software or any other means to prevent copyright infringement.[66] The Court also looked askance at the fact that the Grokster name is obviously a derivative of Napster which was, by then, a known illegal file-sharing service.[67]

While this approach is no doubt consistent with existing law on contributory liability, it has thrown later courts into some confusion about the relevant test to apply to determine contributory liability for digital copyright infringement. For example, in *Capitol Records v ReDigi*, another case involving .mp3 music files, Judge Sullivan in the District Court of the Southern District of New York accepted the litigants' arguments that the "inducement" claim was separate from the "contributory liability" claim.[68] The Ninth Circuit in 2007 characterized contributory liability as comprising two separate categories: (1) actively encouraging – or "inducing" – direct infringement; and (2) distributing a product that is used to infringe copyrights where the product is incapable of substantial non-infringing uses.[69] While both of these approaches are consistent with the law set out in *Grokster*, neither of them seems to characterize contributory liability in the way the Supreme Court did in *Grokster*. The Supreme Court in *Grokster* appeared to regard "inducement" as part of the test for knowingly participating in infringement, rather than as a separate category of secondary liability.

Judges have generally been careful to maintain a safety valve in the operation of the contributory liability doctrine in copyright cases by maintaining the staple article of commerce doctrine derived initially from patent law and first applied in the copyright context by the Supreme Court in *Sony v Universal*.[70] This was the case in which the court held

---

64 545 U.S. 913 (2005).
65 *Id.*, at 1036.
66 *Id.*, at 916, 1036.
67 *Id.*, at 925.
68 *Capitol Records v ReDigi*, 934 F. Supp.2d 640 (2013).
69 See discussion in Ku et al., *supra* note 1, at 412.
70 464 U.S. 417 (1984).

that the makers of the Betamax video recorder were not contributorily liable for copyright infringement, partly because there was little to no primary infringement, and partly on the basis of the staple article of commerce doctrine. Home television audiences were permitted, as a matter of fair use – according to the majority of the Court – to make home recordings of television programs for later viewing.

To the extent that primary infringements were problematic, the Court further held that the manufacturers of staple articles of commerce which may be used to infringe copyrights but are also capable of substantial non-infringing uses, cannot, without more, be held liable for copyright infringement.[71] The court in *Grokster* did not overturn *Sony*.[72] However, the defendants in *Grokster* were unable to avail themselves of the staple article of commerce doctrine because they had taken significant steps to induce the infringements in question.

In the digital age, questions of vicarious liability typically tend to arise alongside questions of contributory liability. *Grokster* is perhaps an unusual example of a case which was predominantly about contributory liability rather than vicarious liability because it relied on inducement. In most digital cases, the facts that support a traditional claim of contributory liability on the basis of knowledge and substantial participation will also support vicarious liability on the basis of direct financial benefit with the ability to monitor and control the infringement.

In *Napster*, for example, the same facts that gave rise to the claims of contributory liability also supported the claim for vicarious liability. The court held that Napster was contributorily liable because it had actual knowledge of specific infringing activities in a situation where it participated in the activities by allowing customers engaging in illegal file sharing to continue their activities with no warnings, or with no threats to deactivate their accounts.[73] On the same facts, Napster was held vicariously liable on the basis that any commercial profits it made would be directly attributable to the amount of infringing file sharing being undertaken[74] in circumstances where it could monitor the file sharing

---

[71] *Id.*, at 442.

[72] *Grokster*, *supra* note 22, at 915 ("Nothing in *Sony* requires courts to ignore evidence of intent to promote infringement if such evidence exists. It was never meant to foreclose rules of fault-based liability derived from the common law").

[73] *A&M Records v Napster*, 239 F.3d 1004, 1017 (2001).

[74] *Id.*, at 1097 ("Napster has a duty to police its system in order to avoid vicarious infringement. Napster can police the system by searching its index for files containing a noticed copyrighted work").

(through its indexing function) and control it (through potentially warning customers and ultimately deactivating their accounts).[75]

As early as 1995, the judicial discussions of contributory versus vicarious liability revolved heavily around the same elements of the factual scenarios confronting the court. In *Netcom*, for example, the court notes that an Internet service provider might be contributorily liable for infringing postings initiated by others because a service provider who obtains notice of infringement (say, through a letter from the copyright holder) and fails to remove the infringing material can be regarded as an active participant in the infringement with knowledge.[76] Such a service provider could further be vicariously liable if it received a financial benefit directly attributable to the infringing content – say, through advertising or membership revenues – in a situation where it had the ability to monitor and remove the infringing material.[77]

The safe harbor provisions of the OCILLA will obviously immunize an online service provider from liability in situations where it had insufficient knowledge of the infringement and acted expeditiously to remove infringing content on notice, *and* in situations where the defendant did not receive a direct financial benefit from the infringement or was not in a position to monitor or control it. However, the OCILLA does not protect a service provider where the elements of contributory or vicarious liability are made out on the facts. In some cases, another defense may be available to a defendant in such a case: for example fair use, which is discussed in more detail below.

2.3.4.2 Online intermediary case studies: contributory and vicarious liability

Some of the post-*Grokster* cases dealing with the potential for secondary liability of online intermediaries are instructive in considering the balance between protecting copyrights and promoting technological innovation in the digital age. In 2007, a pair of cases involving the Perfect 10 erotic digital image service was decided in the Ninth Circuit. In *Perfect 10 v*

---

75 *Id.*

76 *Netcom*, *supra* note 33, at 1373 ("If plaintiffs can prove the knowledge element, Netcom will be liable for contributory infringement since its failure to simply cancel Erlich's infringing message and thereby stop an infringing copy from being distributed worldwide constitutes substantial participation in Erlich's public distribution of the message").

77 This was not the case in *Netcom* where the court held that the defendant was not liable for vicarious infringement: *Id.*, at 1377.

Google,[78] the action involved the Google search engine inline linking to infringing third party websites. In *Perfect 10 v Visa*,[79] on the other hand, the litigation went a step further and involved the electronic payments services that facilitated payment for infringing images available online.

In the *Google* case, the court initially held that it was possible for the contributory liability claim to be made out, but the case was remanded because of the need for further information about the operation of Google's search engine capabilities. On remand, Google was found not to be liable for secondary infringement.[80] By contrast, in the e-payments litigation, the majority of the court in the initial decision held that the e-payments service providers' activities were too far removed from the primary infringements to support any secondary liability claims. This section considers the court's reasoning as to why the secondary liability of a search engine depends on the details of its technical operation while the liability of a payments system is regarded as too far removed from primary infringements to attract secondary liability. It suggests that potentially the majority's reasoning in *Visa* on this point may not withstand close scrutiny.

With respect to the search engine, the Ninth Circuit considered the possibility that Google might be contributorily or vicariously liable for the third party websites' direct infringements of Perfect 10's copyrighted images. The infringements occurred when unauthorized third party websites disseminated copies of Perfect 10's protected images. With respect to the contributory liability claim, the court acknowledged the possibility that contributory liability *could* be attached to a search engine in certain circumstances: "Google could be held contributorily liable if it had knowledge that infringing Perfect 10 images were available using its search engine, could take simple measures to prevent further damage to Perfect 10's copyrighted works, and failed to take such steps".[81] However, on remand Google was not held liable.[82] The original decision held that there no basis for holding Google liable on the vicarious liability claim, so the remanded claim was limited to a discussion of contributory liability.

By contrast, the majority of the Ninth Circuit found that there was no initial basis for holding the e-payments systems liable on any secondary liability basis. Even though the payments systems were utilized to make

---

78 *Supra* note 40.
79 494 F.3d 788 (9th Cir. 2007).
80 *Perfect 10 v Google*, 653 F.3d 976 (2011).
81 Ku et al., *supra* note 1, at 414.
82 *Perfect 10 v Google*, 653 F.3d 976 (2011).

the infringing activities profitable, the majority held that their activities were too far removed from the direct infringements for them to be held accountable for the infringements on a secondary basis. The majority was strident in its holding that it would be inappropriate to attach liability to payments systems for infringing online activities of others: "To find that Defendant's activities fall within the scope of [secondary liability] would require a radical and inappropriate expansion of the existing principles of secondary liability and would violate the public policy of the United States".[83]

With respect to contributory liability, the majority noted that: "The credit card companies cannot be said to materially contribute to the infringement … because they have no direct connection to the infringement".[84] While this may be true, it has never been the test for contributory liability that the defendant has a direct connection with infringement, but rather the defendant must participate in the infringement, with knowledge. It is arguable that payments systems, at least when put on notice by copyright holders, do have knowledge and do participate in infringement by not freezing accounts of copyright pirates.

In terms of the distinction between the *Google* litigation and the litigation involving the e-payments systems, the Ninth Circuit noted that while the search engine itself assists in distribution of infringing content, the payments systems do not.[85] They neither enable Internet users to locate infringing material, nor do they help distribute it.[86] While the payments systems make it easier for third party infringers to *profit* from their infringements, they do not actually contribute to the infringement itself in the sense of copying and distributing infringing material.[87] Of course, technically the Google search engine neither copied nor distributed the images from third party websites. It simply created inline links to those websites. So this distinction between the cases is spurious. The Ninth Circuit further noted that while credit card systems help make infringement profitable, without their involvement in payments, there would be other ways for third parties to profit from the infringement, such as advertising on their websites.[88]

Similarly, with respect to vicarious liability, the court held that while the imposition of such liability on the credit card companies might

---

83 494 F.3d 788, 795 (9th Cir. 2007).

84 *Id.*, at 796.

85 *Id.*

86 *Id.*

87 *Id.*

88 *Id.*, at 797.

remove one of the primary defendants' incentives to infringe, it is not the same as saying those companies are in a position to control the infringement.[89] The ability of the payments systems to block access to payments services was insufficient to give them control over the infringements for vicarious liability purposes according to the court because the "ability to exert financial pressure does not give the Defendants the right or ability to control the actual infringing activity".[90]

In other words, being able to exert pressure over profit margins is not the same as being able to control infringement per se. In conclusion, the court noted that: "For vicarious liability to attach … the defendant must have the right and ability to *supervise* and *control* the infringement, not just affect it, and Defendants do not have this right or ability …".[91] The court did not consider the "direct financial benefit" limb of vicarious liability because it found that the first limb – right and ability to control the activity – was not made out on the facts with respect to the e-payments systems.[92]

The *Google* and *Visa* cases are difficult to reconcile because both services seem relatively far removed from the primary infringements. A search engine merely indexes websites and makes them easier to find while a payments system enables payments for online services. Neither service is established with the aim of infringing copyrights and neither benefits significantly from copyright infringements. Indeed, if this were the test for secondary infringement, the e-payments systems would arguably be more heavily complicit in the primary infringements as they actually profit directly from them. The difficulty of reconciling the cases was noted by Judge Kozinski in his dissent in the *Visa* case:

> According to the majority, "Google may materially contribute to infringement by making it fast and easy for third parties to locate and distribute infringing material, whereas Defendants make it easier for infringement to be *profitable*, which tends to increase financial incentives to infringe, which in turn tends to increase infringement." The majority is mistaken; there is no "additional step". Defendants participate in every credit card sale of pirated images; the images are delivered to the buyer only after defendants approve the transaction and process the payment. This is not just an economic incentive for infringement; it's an essential step in the infringement process …[93]

---

89 *Id.*, at 803.
90 *Id.*, at 804.
91 *Id.*, at 805.
92 *Id.*
93 *Id.*, at 811.

> My colleagues recognize … that helping consumers locate infringing content can constitute contributory infringement, but they consign the means of payment to secondary status … But why is *locating* infringing images more central to infringement than *paying* for them? If infringing images can't be found, there can be no infringement; but if infringing images can't be paid for, there can be no infringement either …[94]

Judge Kozinski emphasized the fact that, contrary to the majority's view, contributory infringement does not rely on direct contact with the infringing activity, but rather on substantial participation in the activity with knowledge of the infringement. He makes the analogy with lending money to a drug dealer in the knowledge that he will use it to finance a drug deal. There is material assistance in the activity even if the money lender never sees the drugs.[95] Judge Kozinski appreciates that the majority's concerns are motivated by a concern about line-drawing between supporting online services and chilling their activities by imposing unreasonable burdens on them. However, he expresses the view that while drawing these lines is always difficult in practice, accepting that online services such as payments systems might have sufficient knowledge of infringement for contributory liability can always be mitigated in practice when applying the second limb of the test: deciding whether they rendered *material* assistance to the infringers.[96]

Judge Kozinski further dissents on the vicarious liability point, noting that the e-payments systems clearly profited directly from infringing activities by taking a cut of the payments attributable to infringing sales of copyrighted works, while they have the ability to cancel access to the system by direct infringers.[97] In particular, the credit card companies have authority under their contracts with merchants to require copyright infringers to remove infringing content from their websites as a condition for accessing the payments systems.[98]

He roundly dismissed the majority's concerns about holding the credit card companies vicariously liable for the activities of the infringing websites:

> [I]t makes no difference that defendants control only the means of payment, not the mechanics of transferring the material … In a commercial environment, distribution and payment are (to use a quaint anachronism) like love

---

94 *Id.*, at 812.
95 *Id.*, at 815.
96 *Id.*
97 *Id.*, at 816.
98 *Id.*

> and marriage – you can't have one without the other. If cards don't process payment, pirates don't deliver booty. The credit cards, in fact, control distribution of the infringing material.[99]

With respect to the majority's concern that e-payments systems can only exert financial pressure on the infringers, and do not have the absolute right or ability to stop the infringement, Judge Kozinski noted that vicarious liability has never required a secondary defendant to have the absolute right to curtail the infringement.[100] Rather, it is sufficient for the defendant to have a practical ability to curtail infringement.[101]

A comparison of the *Google* and *Visa* cases, with particular reference to Judge Kozinski's dissent in the latter, highlights the delicate balance courts are required to strike in the digital age when considering questions of Internet intermediary liability for direct infringements initiated by others. While hosting infringing content may be one issue – and can be addressed by safe harbor provisions – the activities of those service providers further removed from the chain of infringement are more challenging. These situations exemplify the importance of a cyberlaw of the future focusing on the delicate balance between the promotion of innovation in digital technologies and the protection of existing legal rights.

2.3.5 Copyright's Defenses: Fair Use

2.3.5.1 The contours of the fair use defense

An important safety valve that can be utilized in digital copyright litigation to ensure the balance between the promotion of technological innovation on the Internet intermediary side and the protection of copyrights is the fair use defense. While originally a judicial creation,[102] the defense was codified in the 1976 copyright act for the first time.[103] It can now be found in 17 U.S.C. § 107. Despite its statutory placement, the defense retains its equitable rule of reason character that allows judges to be relatively flexible in its application.[104] Without this flexibility, it would

---

99 *Id.*, at 818.

100 *Id.*

101 *Id.*

102 LEAFFER, *supra* note 11, at 487.

103 *Id.*, at 488 ("Although first articulated in case law in the mid-19th century, fair use was not given its first statutory recognition until the 1976 Act").

104 *Id.* ("the fair use defense continues to defy precise definition and remains an ad hoc equitable rule of reason where finding an infringement would undermine the ultimate purpose of copyright law").

be difficult to apply it meaningfully to new situations involving innovative copying and distribution technologies. While some other jurisdictions have more clearly delineated guidelines for excusable copying under "fair dealing" laws,[105] several of these jurisdictions have looked to the United States concept of fair use as providing a more flexible approach to questions of balancing rights and interests in the digital age.

In the United States, fair use is also regarded as an important safeguard for free speech interests and is said to be an important part of the balancing act between freedom of expression and proprietary interests in expression more generally.[106] While the fair use defense, like the OCILLA provisions, is expressed in terms of immunizing a defendant from liability, it is always regarded as an affirmative defense that becomes relevant after the plaintiff has established a prima facie case for copyright infringement.[107] As expressed in § 107, the fair use defense breaks down into two parts – the preamble and the four "fair use factors". The preamble states that:

> Notwithstanding the provisions of Section 106 [the copyright holder's exclusive rights], the fair use of a copyrighted work … for purposes such as criticism, comment, news reporting, teaching (including multiple copies for classroom use), scholarship, or research, is not an infringement of copyright.

The preamble should not be read to imply that any activity that could be described as belonging to one of the listed categories will necessarily be excused as a fair use. These activities are articulated as examples of the kinds of uses that have in the past been typically regarded as fair uses. There are also other specific kinds of use that are not mentioned in the preamble that may well be regarded by courts – and have in the past been regarded by courts – as fair uses. Parody is one example of this.[108] The fact that the uses specified in the preamble are examples of potentially

---

[105] See, for example, Copyright, Designs and Patents Act (1988), Eng., Chapter III.

[106] NEIL NETANEL, COPYRIGHT'S PARADOX, 180–81 (2008) (noting the role of both fair use and the idea/expression dichotomy in copyright law as supposedly protecting First Amendment values).

[107] LEAFFER, *supra* note 11, at 488 ("The defense of fair use becomes relevant only after the plaintiff has made out a prima facie case for copyright infringement by showing copying of the original work and substantial similarity between the works. Once this occurs, the defendant bears the evidentiary burdens of production and persuasion that the infringing use of the copyrighted work was privileged as a fair use").

[108] *Id.*, at 489.

fair uses, but not clear guidelines delineating excused uses of copyright works, is one way in which American fair use law differs significantly from the fair dealing laws in many other countries. In the United Kingdom, for example, specific categories of uses are expressly excused as fair dealing in the copyright legislation.[109] Uses not contemplated by the statute are not fair dealing. The United Kingdom approach has the advantage of greater certainty of application in a given case, but the disadvantage of lesser flexibility.

Following the preamble, § 107 goes on to list the four fair use factors. It is these factors that are the key to determining whether any given use might be regarded as a fair use and thus not a copyright infringement. The four fair use factors are set out in the following terms:

> In determining whether the use made of a work in any particular case is a fair use the factors to be considered shall include –
>
> (1) the purpose and character of the use, including whether such use is of a commercial nature or is for nonprofit educational purposes;
> (2) the nature of the copyrighted work;
> (3) the amount and substantiality of the portion used in relation to the copyrighted work as a whole; and
> (4) the effect of the use upon the potential market for or value of the copyrighted work.

While the section suggests that the four factors are non-exhaustive, courts typically focus on only these factors when determining fair use. However, courts have added judicial glosses to existing factors. For example, the first factor is often analyzed with respect to whether the purpose and character of the defendant's use is "transformative".[110] This issue is taken up in more detail below. The term "transformative" does not appear in the statute but has become a mainstay in judicial discussion of the first factor.[111] The second factor is often analyzed with respect to whether or not the work has been previously published.[112] Again, this is not specifically contemplated in the statute, but it arises in much of the case law.

Courts will sometimes discuss factors one and four together because both relate to the commercialization and effect of the use on the market

---

[109] Copyright, Designs and Patents Act (1988), Eng., Chapter III.

[110] TEHRANIAN, *supra* note 3, at 27–31 (describing the common law genesis of the transformative use aspect of the fourth fair use factor).

[111] *Id.*

[112] PATRY ON COPYRIGHTS, § 10:139.

for, or value of, the copyrighted work.[113] Discussions about factor four in particular can be fraught in the digital age when considering newer market models that have not yet been tested in practice. For example, much of the debate surrounding early digital music file-sharing services was occasioned because the music producers had not yet entered the market and others had availed themselves of the opportunity to do so. In early digital file-sharing cases like *Napster*, courts considered arguments about the effect of the defendant's use on actual or potential markets of the copyright holders. Napster even argued that the ability to engage in free file sharing might actually increase music sales by making more music available to more people who might ultimately buy legitimate copies of the works.[114]

Professor Leaffer has emphasized the problems courts have faced in applying the fair use defense in the context of new digital technologies. In particular, he notes that many of the recent digital fair use decisions create an impression that litigation involving fair use is not the most effective way of solving the issues of balancing new technological innovations against protecting copyrights.[115] One specific problem with relying too heavily on fair use to resolve questions of this balance in the digital age lies within the nature of the litigation process itself. It simply takes too long and costs too much to litigate the cases.

Additionally, the result of litigation with respect to one new technology can ultimately have the effect of regulating an entire industry.[116] Professor Leaffer has suggested that legislatures, rather than courts, are more effective at finding industry-wide solutions to balancing copyrights with technological innovation in reproduction and distribution.[117] However, many legislative solutions, outside the OCILLA safe-harbor provisions for online service providers, have been controversial and ineffective. The debate over SOPA and its ultimate failure to be enacted is a good example of this dynamic in practice.

It may be that ultimately industry solutions are preferable to litigation or legislation. However, in the absence of the threat of litigation or

---

[113] LEAFFER, *supra* note 11, at 495 ("The focus on the economic impact of the use [in factor one] shows this factor's obvious connection with the fourth factor, the effect of the use on the potential market for the copyrighted work").

[114] *A&M Records v Napster*, 239 F.3d 1004, 1017 (2001).

[115] LEAFFER, *supra* note 11, at 507 ("Reviewing the several [fair use] cases involving the new technologies leaves the impression that the litigation process is not capable of solving the issues raised").

[116] *Id.*, at 507.

[117] *Id.*, at 508.

unfavorable legislation, industry participants may not have sufficient incentives to work cooperatively to create an effective balance of interests. For example, industries have worked very effectively together to prevent copyright piracy in terms of online service providers taking affirmative action on receipt of copyright notices, and promulgating terms of service that discourage copyright infringement. However, much of this occurred in the shadow of negotiations over online service provider liability legislation.

2.3.5.2 Digital technology and the four fair use factors

Fair use factors one and four are in many ways the mainstays to deciding digital copyright cases involving the defense. These factors can be problematic in the sense that new disruptive digital technologies can be difficult to evaluate in terms of their impact on the value of, or market for, copyright works under the fourth factor in particular. It can also be challenging, under the first factor, to ascertain when an innovative digital use of a work is transformative or productive. Transformative uses are more likely to be regarded as fair uses than purely personal or consumptive uses. A transformative or productive use is regarded as a use which adds value by creating "new information, new aesthetics, new insights and understandings".[118] Conversely, a non-productive or non-transformative use would arise when "a user copies the material to use it for the same intrinsic purpose for which the copyright owner intended it to be used".[119]

In other words, if I copy my friend's copy of a book, song or movie rather than buying a copy for myself, I have made a non-productive use – a consumptive, or personal, use. I have simply used for myself something that I arguably should have paid for without contributing anything new to anyone else's understanding or enjoyment of the work. On the other hand, if I present the work in a new context, such as creating a musical mash-up or work of fanfiction, I might arguably have engaged in productive or transformative use. There is no statutory requirement that to be a fair use, the use has to be productive or transformative. In one of the leading fair use cases – *Sony v Universal* – purely consumptive, non-transformative uses of the copyrighted works in question were held to be fair uses.[120] That case involved video home-taping of television

---

[118] LEAFFER, *supra* note 11, at 490.

[119] *Id.*

[120] 464 U.S. 417 (1984).

programs for later viewing by consumers. It is also possible that a use, despite being productive or transformative, may not be regarded as a fair use.

Another wrinkle that has arisen in digital age litigation in determining whether a use is transformative for the purposes of the first fair use factor is whether the concept of transformativeness has to apply to the work itself or can also apply to the manner in which the work is presented or perceived. Prior to the digital age, most judicial discussions of transformative use revolved around an actual use of the work itself in terms of changing it into something else. For example, hip hop music often involves remixing multiple works into something new and thus changing the nature of the underlying works themselves. However, a number of digital age fair use cases involve a defendant maintaining the basic nature of the work but simply presenting it in a new digital format. Thumbnail images in search engine results are an obvious example of this. At least two courts have held that the reproduction of the precise unchanged copyrighted image as a thumbnail in search engine results is a transformative use.[121] More recently several courts have held that digitizing literal verbatim copies of books to promote their functionality in terms of things like text searching and access for the print handicapped are transformative in this functional sense.[122] Transformative use in this context is something quite different in quality from transformative use in the previous case law.

The ability of courts to be able to adapt the concept of transformative use in this way to create the necessary balance between promoting technological innovations (such as image search engine capabilities) and copyrights is an advantage of the flexible approach to fair use in the United States. However, the lack of clear guidelines on the relevance of transformative use to the first factor and the definition of "transformativeness" in this context might be unsatisfying as a theoretical matter.

The second fair use factor – the nature of the copyrighted work – has not proved as challenging in practice in the digital world as the first and fourth factors. The second factor is generally applied in a relatively straightforward way with the policy aim of protecting uses of works that might increase the overall fund of information in society.[123] Thus, works that are more scientific or functional in nature tend to receive less

---

[121] *Kelly v ArribaSoft*, 336 F.3d 811 (2003); *Perfect 10 v Google*, 487 F.3d 701 (9th Cir. 2007).

[122] See, for example, *Authors' Guild v HathiTrust*, 902 F. Supp.2d 445 (2012); *Authors' Guild v Google*, 954 F. Supp.2d 282 (2013).

[123] LEAFFER, *supra* note 11, at 497.

protection than works that are more artistic or aesthetic. The law aims to extend on socially beneficial uses of copyrighted works and these uses tend to relate to science and technology more than to arts and entertainment.

In this sense there is a clear relationship between the purposes behind factors one and two of the fair use factors. Factor one has come to focus on the protection as fair use of transformative uses of works, and transformative uses (in the social benefit sense) tend to be uses that increase the store of human knowledge which, in turn, tend to be uses that involve scientific and technological knowledge. Many of the digital age cases involving internet intermediaries revolve around downstream uses by consumers of movies, music and video games. These uses tend to be consumptive for the purposes of the first factor and focus on entertainment value rather than increasing the store of human knowledge. Thus, courts generally hold the uses in, say, music file-sharing cases less likely to be fair use under both factors one and two because of the nature of the use and the nature of the work respectively.

In the past, courts considering factor two have also noted that the fair use privilege may be narrower in the case of unpublished works than published works. This is because courts have proved deferential to the author's right to control at least the first publication of a work.[124] This issue has not arisen in many digital fair use cases partly because of amendments to § 107 to clarify that there is no per se rule barring a finding of fair use with respect to an unpublished work,[125] and largely because most digital cases involve published works. Where online intermediaries are concerned, the cases tend to control reproductions and further disseminations and uses of works uploaded by someone else, rather than publication of unpublished works.

The third fair use factor – the amount and substantiality of the portion of the work used – raises its own issues, but most of those issues are not specific to digital copyright cases, at least in the sense that factors one and four raise special challenges of identifying the impact of new digital markets on the value of a work. As Professor Leaffer notes, one of the more significant issues generally raised by factor three is the relationship between this factor and the "substantial similarity" question that is part of the initial infringement inquiry.[126] While the question of substantial

---

124 *Id.*, at 498.

125 17 U.S.C. § 107 ("... The fact that a work is unpublished shall not itself bar a finding of fair use if such finding is made upon consideration of all the above factors").

126 *Id.*, at 499.

similarity has to be established by the plaintiff as part of making out its prima facie case of infringement, the question of "amount and substantiality of the portion used" casts the burden on the defendant. In this context, the defendant must establish that it did not use more of the work than was necessary for the specific fair use purposes claimed in any given case.[127]

Again, while not specific to the digital age, it is important to note that questions of amount and substantiality have both a quantitative and a qualitative dimension. One can take a portion of a work that is quantitatively small but still exceeds the fair use privilege if that small portion comprises the essence of the work. In the well-known Supreme Court case of *Harper & Row v Nation Enterprises*,[128] the defendant's taking of only 300 words from an approximately 200,000 word manuscript was regarded as excessive because the small passage comprised the heart of the work. Taking the heart of the work in this way may effectively destroy – or at least significantly negatively impact – the copyright holder's ability to exploit the work commercially.

Unlike the second and third factors, the fourth factor has proved problematic in the digital age for much the same reasons as the first factor. Because the fourth factor relies on an analysis of the effect of the defendant's use on the potential market for, or value of, the copyrighted work, it often involves significant crystal-gazing on behalf of the judiciary. While this is true of non-digital cases, advances in digital innovations occur so rapidly that it is very difficult for courts to make these determinations in a timely manner. Additionally, those who create innovations in communications technology are often not those who are focused on digital content production. At least historically this has been the case.

For example, while the recording industry and the movie industry were focused on developing and distributing hard copy CDs and DVDs in the early days of digital technology, other innovators outside these industries were developing online file-sharing technologies. Thus, Napster, for example, beat the recording industry to the online file-sharing market. Subsequently, the recording industry has mastered a large portion of that market through digital music distribution services such as iTunes. However, when the Napster case came before the courts, it was not clear how, when, or if, an authorized digital music distribution model might develop, and what its cost structures would look like. Thus, asking a

---

127 *Id.*

128 471 U.S. 539, 569 (1985).

court to determine the likely impact of Napster's activities on an as-yet undetermined market in the hands of the copyright holders was a tall order.

As Professor Leaffer has noted, courts will generally proscribe an activity that tends to threaten the incentives for copyright protection: in other words, a use that diminishes the potential sale of the work in the hands of the copyright holder.[129] In this sense, uses that substitute for the copyright holder's use are more of a threat than uses that complement a copyright holder's use. Nevertheless, it is often difficult to determine whether a use is a potential substitute for the copyright holder's efforts or complementary to it if that use is something completely new. One might think, for example, that a search engine that indexes digital images and makes them easier to find is a complementary use of the work because it enables potential customers to locate the copyright holder's website more easily than would otherwise be the case. However, as the *Kelly v ArribaSoft*[130] and *Perfect 10 v Google*[131] cases demonstrate, copyright holders do not always view such uses as complementary.

One reason for this view is that copyright holders may be generally leery of any such use in that it is just as easy for a search engine to direct an Internet user to an infringing website as to the legitimate copyright holder's website. However, this was not the express question under consideration with respect to the thumbnail images utilized in the search engines in either of these cases. That was rather a question of secondary liability for direct infringements with respect to inline linking. In *Perfect 10 v Google*, the copyright holder raised an argument that the thumbnail images generated by the Google search engine might prove to be a substitute in the market for cellphone wallpaper with respect to the protected images. However, ultimately the court did not accept that argument.

Even that relatively inconsequential example of the use of erotic images as cellphone wallpaper shows that potential market harm is very difficult to ascertain in practice in the digital age. There is really no empirically accurate way of either party demonstrating which markets are more or less likely to materialize in a fast-moving area like digital technology where what is hot one day is prehistoric the next. Some ideas that seem like they have significant commercial potential never come to fruition while others that seem objectively pointless, succeed beyond

---

129 LEAFFER, *supra* note 11, at 500.

130 336 F.3d 311 (9th Cir. 2003).

131 508 F.3d 1146 (9th Cir. 2007).

anyone's wildest expectations. Who would have predicted the success of Twitter, for example, when it was first launched? Or that Facebook would overtake MySpace as the premier online social network?

One aspect of the fourth fair use factor that has proved helpful to copyright holders in digital cases has been the fact that courts are only required to accept a "meaningful likelihood of future harm [to a potential market] on a preponderance of the evidence".[132] At least with respect to entertainment-focused works like digital music and movies, courts have tended to be relatively deferential to the needs of the copyright holders than to those engaged in downstream uses of their works.

2.3.5.3 Case studies: online intermediaries and fair use

Digital fair use cases involving online intermediaries have tended to favor copyright holders, particularly where the work in question is predominantly of entertainment value (movies, music) and the use is predominantly consumptive or non-transformative. In these cases, even where the evidence is equivocal, courts have been prepared to assume that a defendant's use is commercial for the purposes of factor one and will likely have a negative impact on a future market for the work for the purposes of factor four. For example, in the *Napster* litigation, even though Napster was not making a commercial profit from consumer file sharing at the time the litigation was commenced, and even though the recording industries were not in the online distribution market, copyright infringement was found. Of course, in *Napster* the infringement was of a secondary nature because Napster itself engaged in no actual copying or distribution but merely facilitated copying and distribution by others.

However, in the case of *UMG Recordings v MP3.com*,[133] the District Court in the Southern District of New York did not accept a defendant intermediary's fair use argument where the intermediary itself engaged in the copying and distribution of the plaintiff's works. Here, the defendant had established what it conceived of as a "space shifting" service for owners of compact disc recordings of musical works. If a user established that it owned a legal copy of a work, the defendant would allow the user to access the work from multiple devices, streamed to the user from its own servers. The defendant relied on the *Sony v Universal* conception of legitimate personal consumptive uses as fair uses in arguing that its service allowed its customers to make fair uses of works

---

[132] LEAFFER, *supra* note 11, at 501.

[133] 92 F. Supp.2d 349 (S.D.N.Y. 2000).

they legitimately owned. The customers were simply making uses in locations other than the location of their legitimately purchased CD of the work.

The court did not accept this argument, easily dispensing with the defendant's arguments involving fair use factors two and three. With respect to factor two, the court noted that the musical works under consideration were not the kinds of works generally given fair use leeway. They were not "factual or descriptive work more amenable to 'fair use'".[134] With respect to factor three, the court noted that as the defendant copied and distributed the entirety of the plaintiffs' works, the amount and substantiality of the use easily cut against fair use.[135] In terms of the first fair use factor, the court held that the uses made by the defendant were not transformative in any sense of the word. The defendant did not infuse the works with new meanings or new understandings. It simply provided a "space shift" so that its customers could avoid lugging around their CD collections to enjoy the music they had purchased.[136]

Importantly, with respect to the fourth fair use factor, the court considered potential markets the plaintiffs might want to exploit. The court noted that the defendant's services "invade plaintiffs' statutory right to license their copyrighted sound recordings to others for reproduction".[137] By way of counter-argument, the defendant noted that not only had the plaintiff failed to adduce sufficient evidence that it intended to exploit this market itself, but also that the defendant's services were complementary to the plaintiffs' services, rather than substitutes for them, because no one could use the defendant's service unless it first bought a legitimate copy of the plaintiffs' protected works.[138]

This was very much a situation where a court was required to look at digital markets that had not yet developed and formulate policy and theoretical bases on which to decide how the market might develop in the future. The court was faced with competing evidence as to how significant the plaintiffs' efforts had been to develop a licensing market for digital music distribution. It was further faced with the theoretical question of what it means to protect the copyright holders' proprietary interests in the context contemplated in factor four. In the final analysis, the court took the view that copyright "is not designed to afford

---

134 *Id.*, at 351–52.
135 *Id.*, at 352.
136 *Id.*
137 *Id.*
138 *Id.*

consumer protection or convenience but … to protect the copyright holders' proprietary interests".[139]

While it does seem sensible to protect prospective licensing markets to copyright holders at least in the early days of fast-moving digital technologies, the distinction between consumer interests and copyright holders' interests seems a little spurious on close examination. If the aim of the fourth fair use factor is to incentivize creativity in society overall, the ability of consumers to access works – particularly works they have already paid for – should be an important aspect of this motivation. If licensing – or other – markets for existing works, including works of entertainment, fail to develop because they are reserved for copyright holders who may or may not choose to exploit them absent the threat of someone else beating them to market, downstream creation may be disincentivized.

The threat of disincentivizing creation may have been absent in *UMG Recordings* as the works in question were already openly accessible to those interested in them and could be enjoyed by those people anywhere they could take a CD player. So in some ways this may have been an easy case. However, the suggestion that courts should generally defer to intellectual property rights under the fourth factor over and above consumer interests may be problematic in other contexts.

Of course, none of the fair use factors is ever considered in isolation and it may be that the *UMG* court took the approach it did with respect to factor four because the other factors, at least in its opinion, weighed so heavily against fair use. It is important that future courts focus on the interplay between the factors. Sometimes in digital cases, factor four seems to be given disparate weight in the analysis,[140] and it is important that the analysis of this factor does not become separated from its relationship with the other fair use factors.

An interesting recent development in digital copyright law is the increasing volume of cases involving the digitization of books.[141] In recent cases involving literary texts, the fair use analysis has tended to operate – at least in recent years – in favor of the defendants.[142] This is likely because of the kinds of cases that arise with respect to digital

---

[139] *Id.*

[140] LEAFFER, *supra* note 11, at 500 ("The case law frequently states that [the fourth fair use] factor is the single most important element of fair use").

[141] See discussion in Jacqueline Lipton, *Copyright, Plagiarism, and Emerging Norms in Digital Publishing*, 16 VANDERBILT JOURNAL OF ENTERTAINMENT AND TECHNOLOGY LAW 585, (2014).

[142] *Id.*

books. Most of them are not about purely consumptive file sharing or distribution, but rather involve some kind of socially beneficial purpose. The cases that have been litigated in recent years have revolved around situations like the Google Book Project which attempts to digitize much of the world's literature, including much out-of-print literature and orphan works. Other notable cases have involved the digitization of books by libraries to enhance access for those with print disabilities,[143] and the creation of university course packs.[144]

In all of these situations, the defendant may have some commercial profit motives. For example, course packs are not free and students pay admission fees to attend university in any event. Even Google monetizes its services through some retail book sales as well as advertising programs. However, overall the copying and distribution by these kinds of online intermediaries seems to be of a different quality than that of music file-sharing services in terms of the social benefits they provide. Thus, maybe courts are justified in taking a more deferential approach to these kinds of fair uses.

The Google Book project revolves around a plan by search engine giant Google to digitize as many books as possible for free and easy search by the general public.[145] Later iterations of the program also included a more commercial prospect for Google under which it sells e-books to consumers under its Google Play program,[146] much like Amazon's Kindle and Apple's iBookstore. The digitization process involves the creation of copies of large volumes of copyrighted material as well as public domain material and orphan works – works that are copyrighted but for which the author cannot be located.[147]

The social benefits of this program are significant, and were largely balanced against concerns of copyright holders in a settlement agreement with the Association of American Publishers in 2012. The settlement included provisions that allow works to be removed from the program on request. However, the Authors' Guild, representing individual authors, continues its legal battle against Google for copyright infringement, and a

---

143 *Authors' Guild v HathiTrust*, 902 F. Supp.2d 445 (2014).

144 *Cambridge University Press v Becker*, 863 F. Supp.2d 1190 (2012).

145 See Wikipedia, *Google Books Library Project* (available at http://en.wikipedia.org/wiki/Google_Books_Library_Project, last viewed on August 13, 2013).

146 See https://play.google.com/store/books?hl=en, last viewed on July 11, 2013.

147 LEAFFER, *supra* note 11, 231.

fair use defense by Google which was initially upheld in the Second District Court has, at the time of this writing, been appealed.

In the Second Circuit decision, Judge Chen held that Google's use of the literary works was highly transformative under the first fair use factor, noting that:

> Google Books digitizes books and transforms expressive text into a comprehensive word index that helps readers, scholars, researchers, and others find books. Google Books has become an important tool for libraries and librarians and cite-checkers as it helps to identify and find books. The use of book text to facilitate search through the display of snippets is transformative.[148]

This approach to transformative use in a functional sense is very similar to the approaches taken in the thumbnail image search context in *Kelly v ArribaSoft* and *Perfect 10 v Google*.[149] Even though the defendants made literal verbatim copies of entire works, and did not change them to add new insights in the traditional sense of transformativeness, the functionality of use was transformative. Judge Chen held that the first fair use factor cut in favor of Google even though it operated for commercial purposes, the other limb to be considered in factor one analyses. In other words, transformative functionality here outweighed Google's commercial purpose.

With respect to the second fair use factor, Judge Chen held that even though the literary works went to the heart of copyright protection as including many fictional and purely artistic work, the works were published works and already available to the public, so the factor cut in favor of Google.[150] The third factor cut "slightly" against Google because it copied full verbatim texts, even though it limited the portion available in search results.[151] However, the fourth factor weighed heavily in favor of Google because its digitations of the books, according to Judge Chen, were likely to increase awareness of the books and thus potentially increase sales.[152]

Another case involving a similar service provided by Google was the *HathiTrust* litigation which involved a book digitization scheme that was to benefit the public in a number of ways. A consortium of university libraries contracted with Google to digitize millions of books for the

---

148 954 F. Supp.2d 282, 291 (2013).

149 See discussion in Part 2.3.2, *supra*.

150 954 F. Supp.2d 282, 292 (2013).

151 *Id.*

152 *Id.*, at 292–93.

purposes of: (a) full text searches; (b) preservation; and (c) access by people with certified print disabilities.[153] In October of 2012, Judge Baer in the District Court in New York held that this project constituted a fair use.[154] With respect to the first fair use factor, the court was able to determine a number of ways in which the purpose and character of the defendants' use leaned towards fair use. They included the benefits to researchers in identifying relevant works more easily, the benefits to libraries in preventing works from deterioration, and the ability of print-handicapped people to access works more effectively.[155] With respect to the transformative nature of the use, the court followed the *Perfect 10 v Google* ruling in holding that even a use that does not actually change an existing work but rather changes the purpose for which the work is used may be regarded as transformative under the first fair use factor.[156] One of the transformative purposes in this case, for example, was identified by the court as superior research capabilities.[157] This is a transformative use in the same sense that search engines allowing easier identification of, and access to, a copyrighted work was transformative in *Kelly v Arriba Soft* and *Perfect 10 v Google*.

With respect to the second fair use factor, the court was faced with a dilemma in the sense that the majority of the works in question comprised fiction rather than non-fiction. Fiction is more of an entertainment work than an academic or informational work, and thus one might assume that the second fair use factor would cut against the defendants here. However, the court looked to earlier judicial precedents on the relationship between the first and second fair use factor and noted authority that where a use is transformative under factor one, the court should not rely too heavily on the second factor as such reliance would be unlikely to separate fair use from infringement.[158]

As with the second factor, at first glance it would appear that the third fair use factor would cut against the defendants' claims of fair use.

---

153 *Authors' Guild v HathiTrust*, WL 603193 (S.D.N.Y.), 3 (2013) ("For works with known authors, Defendants use the works within the HDL in three ways: (1) full-text searches; (2) preservation; and (3) access for people with certified print disabilities").

154 *Id.*

155 *Id.*, at 15–17.

156 *Id.*, at 16.

157 *Id.*

158 *Id.*, at 18 ("However, where a use is transformative, the nature of the copyrighted work is not likely to 'separate the fair use sheep from the infringing goats'").

However, the court held that the third factor should not be weighed against the defendants because it was necessary for them to copy entire manuscripts in order for the system to work, and to achieve its transformative, socially beneficial, purposes.[159] As with the analysis of factor two, the court was prepared to grant the defendants wide fair use leeway under factor three because of the transformative use made in respect of the factor one analysis.

As usual, the fourth factor was the most difficult to apply, particularly with respect to an innovative new digital service. The court expressly articulated this fact by noting that "the facts here may on some levels be without precedent".[160] However, in the final analysis the court relied on the relationship between the first and fourth fair use factors in holding that the defendants could avail themselves of the fair use defense: "I cannot imagine a definition of fair use that would not encompass the transformative uses made by the Defendants' [Mass Digitization Project] and would require that I terminate this invaluable contribution to the progress of science and the cultivation of the arts that at the same time effectuates the ideals espoused by the [Americans with Disabilities Act]".[161]

In the context of the fourth factor, the plaintiffs mounted some fairly compelling arguments to support their contention that the defendants' digitization project was a substitute for, rather than a complement to, uses the plaintiffs may choose to make of their works. They argued: (1) that each book digitized by the defendants could substitute for a book sold by the copyright holders and thus result in a lost sale;[162] (2) that the defendants' digitization process caused security risks to plaintiffs that could result in unauthorized copying;[163] and (3) that the defendants' project undermined licensing opportunities for the plaintiffs.[164]

The court dismissed each of these arguments. With respect to the first argument, the court stated that even the purchase of additional copies of the plaintiffs' works would not have provided the transformative services – such as print disabled access and full-text searches – that the defendants' project offered.[165] On the second point, the court noted that the

---

[159] *Id.*, at 19 ("Here, entire copies were necessary to fulfill Defendants' purposes of facilitation of searches and access for print-disabled individuals").

[160] *Id.*, at 22.

[161] *Id.*

[162] *Id.*, at 19.

[163] *Id.*, at 19–20.

[164] *Id.*, at 20.

[165] *Id.*, at 19.

evidence on security risks was equivocal at best, and it accepted the evidence of the defendants' security experts over the plaintiffs' evidence of security risks.[166] Finally, the court took the view that the plaintiffs' characterization of lost licensing opportunities was "pure conjecture".[167]

This reasoning on the third argument is particularly interesting from the point of view of the development of the law of online intermediary liability. The arguments here may be usefully contrasted with the reasoning in *UMG Recordings* in which the court readily accepted the plaintiffs' argument that an innovative "space-shifting" service provided by the defendant was encroaching on potential licensing markets.[168]

In terms of the encroachment of the defendant into a potential licensing market which the plaintiffs might otherwise exploit, the *UMG* court noted that: "even if the copyright holder had not yet entered the new market in issue ... a copyright holder's 'exclusive' rights, derived from the Constitution and the Copyright Act, include the right, within broad limits, to curb the development of such a derivative market by refusing to license a copyrighted work or by doing so only on terms the copyright owner finds acceptable".[169] This view may be contrasted with the *HathiTrust* court's citing of an earlier case: "Were a court automatically to conclude in every case that potential licensing revenues were impermissibly impaired simply because the secondary user did not pay a fee for the right to engage in the use, the fourth factor would *always* favor the copyright owner".[170]

It would appear that the key distinction between the two cases is the characterization of the defendants' use of the plaintiffs' works under factor one of the fair use test. While the use in *UMG Recordings* was regarded as non-transformative, the use in *HathiTrust* was transformative. Simply allowing consumers to enjoy something they had already paid for in another physical location did not meet the factor one transformativeness bar, while allowing full-text searches and disabled access to works was regarded as transformative, at least in a functional sense.

As noted above, much of the court's ultimate fair use result on factor four in *HathiTrust* – not to mention factors two and three – hinged on the fact that the defendants' use was regarded as transformative under the first fair use factor. It may be that in these "digital innovation" cases, we

---

166 *Id.*, at 20.

167 *Id.*

168 See discussion in Part 2.3.5.3., *supra*.

169 92 F. Supp.2d 349, 352 (2000).

170 *Authors' Guild v HathiTrust*, WL 603193 (S.D.N.Y.), 3, 20 (2013) (citing *Bill Graham* case, 448 F.3d 614, citation omitted).

are beginning to see the emergence of a "one factor" fair use test, and the decisive factor will be the first fair use factor. Even when arguments exist that the defendants' activities have encroached on the value of, or potential market for, the copyright work, a transformative use seems to trump all other fair use considerations. As noted by the *HathiTrust* court, "A copyright holder cannot preempt a transformative market".[171]

The *HathiTrust* reasoning on fair use may be contrasted with the immediately preceding decision in *Cambridge University Press v Becker* in which representatives of the academic publishing industry failed on their claims of copyright infringement with respect to Georgia State University's digitization of their works to make electronic course packs.[172] As with *HathiTrust*, the court in *Cambridge* held that the copying was excused by the fair use defense. Decisive factors were the non-profit educational motives of the university and the informational nature of the works copied.[173] However, in this case, factor four was a much more significant issue than perhaps was the case in *HathiTrust* and some of the earlier digital intermediary cases. The court in *Cambridge* spent a lot of time discussing the commercial impact of the university's coursepacks on the licensing revenues of the plaintiffs. The difference in reasoning between *Cambridge* and some of the other digital fair use cases may be that this was a case in which a commercial licensing scheme was already in place for at least some of the works in question, so the court was not projecting into the impact of the defendant's actions a non-existent potential market for the plaintiffs' work. Additionally, the defendant's use of the plaintiffs' works in *Cambridge* was non-transformative.[174] It satisfied the first fair use criterion because of its non-profit educational nature.[175]

Factor one was easily disposed of by the court with respect to the non-profit educational purposes of the university in creating the coursepacks. Even though the defendant's use of the works was non-transformative, neither was it a commercial use according to the court. Thus it could be distinguished from cases involving for-profit services

---

171 *Id.*

172 *Cambridge University Press v President of Georgia State University*, 863 F. Supp.2d 1190 (2012).

173 *Id.*, at 1260 ("A review of the fair use factors in this case shows that factor one strongly favors Defendants, factor two favors Defendants, factor three favors Plaintiffs, and factor four strongly favors Plaintiffs").

174 *Id.*, at 1224.

175 *Id.*, at 1225.

making coursepacks at the behest of a university.[176] With respect to the second fair use factor, even though the works in question were books, none of them was fiction. They were all academic and informational texts and thus the fair use privilege was more likely to apply to them than purely fictional/entertainment-based texts.[177] Under the third fair use factor, the court noted that the amount taken from the original works was relatively small – averaging about 10 per cent over all works copied.[178] This amount was regarded as reasonable with respect to the purposes for which the copies were made – classroom instructional use[179] – for a number of the works, although the court engaged in specific case-by-case determinations with respect to each work.

The factor four analysis again proved a challenge for the court. The court started out by noting that even though the burden of proof of fair use is on the defendant, the factor should weigh against the defendant "only when the harm [to the plaintiff] is significant".[180] After a relatively exhaustive summary of the application of all of these issues that potentially arise under factor four, the court concluded that: "there is no persuasive evidence that Plaintiff's ability to publish high quality scholarly books would be appreciably diminished by the modest relief from academic permissions payments which is at issue in this case. There is certainly no evidence that a modest reduction would impact the desire or the ability of academic authors to publish new works. Making small free excerpts available to students would further the spread of knowledge".[181] However, in cases where a licensing regime was available for portions of a textbook, the court held that licensing fees should have been paid with respect to certain of the books.[182]

Having examined a series of digital intermediary fair use cases, one can easily see the central importance of factors one and four of the fair use inquiry as well as their relationship to each other. Contrasting *Cambridge* with some of the other cases demonstrates that the factor four analysis is in some ways easier and in some ways more complex when a licensing mechanism for the copyright works is already in place. Where such a scheme exists, the court needs to consider why the defendant did

---

[176] *Id.*, at 1224.
[177] *Id.*, at 1225.
[178] *Id.*, at 1229–30.
[179] *Id.*, at 1235.
[180] *Id.*
[181] *Id.*, at 1242.
[182] *Id.*, at 1237–38 (on relevance of availability of licensing schemes to fair use analysis).

not avail itself of the scheme, and that puts more pressure on the other fair use factors in the hands of the defendant. However, where a licensing scheme is not already in place, courts are arguably trapped between a rock and a hard place. Contrasting the analyses in *UMG* and *HathiTrust* on factor four, while a court cannot assume that any use not paid for by the defendant is automatically an infringement, it likewise cannot assume that the copyright holder would not have ultimately exploited the market for itself. A lot of this analysis will be crystal-ball gazing in cases where there is insufficient evidence of the plaintiff's plans to enter a new market. In many cases, a plaintiff will not even think to enter into a new market without the pressure exerted by a new technologist potentially – or actually – beating it to the market (as was arguably the case with digital file sharing in *Napster* and space-shifting in *UMG Recordings*). How quickly would copyright holders of musical recordings have worked to establish legitimate digital distribution methods without the pressure of services like Napster and MP3.com?

A comparison of the fair use cases involving online intermediaries evidences the vital role played by such intermediaries in the development of innovations in information-sharing technologies. However, it also shows the risks taken by those intermediaries when their services impact the intellectual property rights of others. The fair use defense is one legal mechanism – like the OCILLA safe harbors – for attempting to strike a balance between enhancing innovation in new digital technologies and protecting digital intellectual property rights.

2.3.6 Copyright's Defenses: First Sale

Until recently, the first sale defense has not been particularly relevant to digital issues. However, new innovations in digital technology are bringing this position into question. The main reason why the defense has not typically applied in digital cases is that digital transactions have generally involved licenses of content rather than sales. Newer online intermediaries are attempting to create "sale-like" transactions with respect to digital content that may ultimately lead to courts accepting that digital transactions can be sales rather than licenses.

The first sale defense is set out in § 109(a) of the copyright act and relates specifically to the exclusive "distribution right" in § 106. Section 109(a) provides that:

> Notwithstanding the provisions of section 106(3), the owner of a particular copy or phonorecord lawfully made under this title, or any person authorized

> by such owner, is entitled, without the authority of the copyright owner, to sell or otherwise dispose of the possession of that copy or phonorecord.

In strict terms, first sale probably should be described as a "doctrine" rather than a "defense" because it immunizes the defendant from liability by creating an entitlement to onsell a copy of a work lawfully made. However, in practice – like fair use – it tends to operate as a defense because it is considered after the plaintiff has established a prima facie case of infringement of the distribution right and the burden shifts to the defendant to establish the availability of the first sale doctrine.

First sale is also referred to as "exhaustion" because the application of the doctrine exhausts the rights of the copyright holder with respect to a given copy of the work.[183] At the international level the exhaustion doctrine has proved highly contentious and countries have failed to reach agreement as to whether a foreign sale of a work will exhaust the copyright holder's rights with respect to that copy. The United States Supreme Court definitively answered this question with respect to American law in the 2013 decision in *Kirtsaeng v John Wiley*,[184] holding that a foreign sale would satisfy the requirements of § 109(a). This decision allowed a student to import legitimately purchased foreign editions of textbooks, sold at a lower price overseas, into the United States for a profit without infringing copyright.

The aim of the first sale doctrine is to prevent copyright holders from negatively impacting the development of downstream markets with respect to legitimately purchased copies of works. It allows the development of secondhand markets in books, music and movies that are legitimately sold in hard copy – for example, CDs and DVDs. Where, however, the content is licensed over a network, first sale has been thought not to apply because there is no actual sale. Even with respect to some hard copies of digital works (such as software sold on storage devices such as CDs), courts have upheld license terms that state the work was merely licensed rather than sold in the first place, thus depriving the putative purchaser of the first sale defense if she wants to onsell her copy of the software.[185]

---

[183] LEAFFER, *supra* note 11, at 328 ("once the work is lawfully sold or even transferred gratuitously, the copyright owner's interest in the material object, the copy or phonorecord, is exhausted; the owner of that copy can then dispose of it as he sees fit").

[184] 133 S. Ct. 1351 (2013).

[185] LEAFFER, *supra* note 11, at 329 ("The second-hand trade in genuine (as distinct from counterfeit) software products is a 'big little business,' and is

In an apocryphal tale which turns out probably not to be true, actor Bruce Willis attracted media attention for allegedly being upset that he was unable to transfer the content of his digital iTunes library to his children via testamentary disposition because the works were merely licensed to him. He didn't own copies of any of them.[186] Whether or not this story is true, it is accurate to say that digital content tends to be licensed rather than sold to consumers so the first sale doctrine is generally not available.

Another reason why the first sale doctrine – at least at first glance – appears not to be readily applicable to digital content is that where content is putatively purchased by downloading it, rather than purchasing a physical copy of it, there is no actual copy physically *transferred* to the consumer. What the consumer actually obtains is a new copy of the work created via electronic transmission, not a transfer of a physical copy from the original owner to the transferee.[187]

This was the heart of the issue faced by Judge Richard Sullivan in the District Court of the Southern District of New York in *Capitol Records v ReDigi*.[188] In this case, an enterprising intermediary tried to create a secondhand market in digital copies of musical works by mimicking what a sale would look like with respect to digitally downloaded content. The ReDigi software, when downloaded by a consumer, analyzed the consumers' computer to build a list of digital music files potentially for sale. The user could only include files purchased from iTunes or another

---

coming under increasing legal fire from major software vendors. Typically, these enterprising resellers invoke 'first sale,' asserting that the firms and individuals from whom they bought their wares were themselves lawful purchasers. The manufacturers respond that the copies in question were never sold, merely 'licensed.' As evidence, they point to various terms in the 'shrink-wrap' agreements that accompany these software products when they are made available by or under the authority of their copyright owners, including 'end user license agreements' ('EULAs')").

[186] Brandon Griggs, *Can Bruce Willis Leave His iTunes Music to His Kids?*, September 4, 2012, CNN TECH (available at http://www.cnn.com/2012/09/03/tech/web/bruce-willis-itunes/, last viewed on June 23, 2014).

[187] LEAFFER, *supra* note 11, at 3313–32 ("Digital transmissions of copyrighted works over the Internet do not comfortably fit within the constraints of the first sale doctrine. The principal reason is that the first sale doctrine is restricted to the transfer of physical copies of the work and provides no defense to infringements of the reproduction right. Unlike transactions where a tangible copy changes hands, an Internet transmission results in a reproduction of the work, through the electronic transmission of a new copy of the work to its recipients").

[188] *Capitol Records v ReDigi*, 934 F. Supp.2d 640 (2013).

Redigi user, thereby ensuring the copies were lawfully downloaded by users in the first place. Users were then able to upload eligible music files to ReDigi's "Cloud Locker" – basically a server where ReDigi stored files available for "sale". If the user sought to sell the copy of the file, the ReDigi software deleted all traces of the file from the user's computer and transferred a copy of the file to the "purchaser". ReDigi argued that this amounted to creating a secondhand market in digital music and should be excused from copyright infringement liability under both the fair use and first sale doctrines.

Judge Sullivan accepted that the plaintiff copyright holders had made out a prima facie case of infringement by ReDigi of their reproduction and distribution rights.[189] He did not accept ReDigi's first sale or fair use arguments. With respect to fair use, the result was perhaps unsurprising. Under the first factor, the court was not convinced there was anything transformative about ReDigi's use of the music files.[190] The use was also commercial, further mitigating against the first factor.[191] The second factor unsurprisingly weighed against ReDigi for the same reasons as in *UMG Recordings* and *Napster*. Music files are pure entertainment works close to the core of copyright protection.[192] Likewise the third factor worked against ReDigi because the copies made were of entire works.[193] Finally, with respect to factor four, the court held that the copies made by ReDigi were clear market substitutes for the copyright holder's property and were sold at a lower price, thereby diverting customers from legitimate markets.[194]

The first sale arguments are more interesting for the purposes of this discussion. Judge Sullivan noted that the first sale defense is limited to infringements of the distribution right and cannot excuse infringement of the reproduction right. Where, as here, the defendant actually made unlawful copies of a work on its own servers, the first sale defense was not applicable.[195] Further, as an "unlawful reproduction" of the copyright holder's works, the copies were not entitled to be regarded as having been "lawfully made under [Title 17]" for the purposes of a § 109(a) analysis.[196] In this vein, Judge Sullivan noted:

---

189 *Id.*
190 *Id.*, at 653–54.
191 *Id.*
192 *Id.*, at 654.
193 *Id.*
194 *Id.*
195 *Id.*, at 655–56.
196 *Id.*

> [T]he first sale defense is limited to material items, like records, that the copyright owner put into the stream of commerce. Here, ReDigi is not distributing such material items; rather, it is distributing *reproductions* of the copyrighted code embedded in new material objects, namely, the ReDigi server … and its users' hard drives. The first sale defense does not cover this any more than it covered the sale of cassette recordings of vinyl records in a bygone era.[197]

While this analysis is logical, it suggests that there is no way that digital technology could ever emulate first sales of content. As we move into the digital age, copyright content users are unable to engage in secondhand market activities that were largely taken for granted in the pre-digital world. It obviously was not the intention of the drafters of the copyright act that when a new technology challenged the operation of accepted first sale paradigms, the first sale defense would cease to exist in large market sectors. However, it is likely not the job of the courts to remedy this problem. Rather it should be a task for Congress to redress the potential imbalance caused by the unintended loss of the first sale defense in digital markets. This was expressly recognized by Judge Sullivan in addressing the defendant's argument that the court should be persuaded to reconceptualize the operation of the first sale defense to meet the realities of new digital technologies:

> [W]hile technological change may have rendered Section 109(a) unsatisfactory to many contemporary observers and consumers, it has not rendered it ambiguous. The statute plainly applies to the lawful owner's "particular" phonorecord, a phonorecord that by definition cannot be uploaded and sold on ReDigi's website … [a]mendment of the Copyright Act in line with ReDigi's proposal is a legislative prerogative that courts are unauthorized and ill-suited to attempt.[198]

With respect to ReDigi's argument that this reading of § 109(a) effectively excludes digital works from the defense altogether, Judge Sullivan noted that a lawful owner of a digital copy of a work can still sell the copy and thus take advantage of the first sale defense. However, the task of selling the particular copy is more difficult because the copy has to be sold along with the physical device that stores it: for example, a computer hard disk, iPod or other memory device onto which the file was originally downloaded.[199]

---

197 *Id.*, at 655.
198 *Id.*
199 *Id.*, at 656.

The judge emphasized the point that while this limitation would clearly make it more difficult to resell a downloaded digital copy than a copy purchased, say, on a CD, the first sale defense has not ceased to exist with respect to downloaded digital copies.[200] It would be interesting to see whether, in fact, it is possible to sell a hard disc or iPod containing digital content, like digital music, consistent with the license terms under which the music was originally purchased. However, that is arguably a matter of contract law rather than the first sale defense. It has always been possible – even in the world of physical copies – to negate first sale through license terms.[201]

Writing before the judgment in *ReDigi*, Professor Leaffer summed up a number of the key concerns with first sale in the digital age:

> The question remains whether the first sale doctrine should be retooled to reflect the realities of the digital age and be made to apply to digital transmissions. Some have argued for a statutory change or a rule permitting the transfer of an electronic work to a single party so long as the sender deletes the copy of the work within a reasonable time. Whether this would … be wise from a policy standpoint is another question. The crux of the matter is that physical copies are inherently different than information in digital formats, and the economic effect of this difference is significant. Physical copies degrade over time, whereas digital information does not. Moreover, works in digital form can be reproduced flawlessly and be disseminated globally at little cost and with low visibility. Thus, a digital first sale would affect the market for the original to a greater degree than transfers of physical copies.[202]

Despite the *ReDigi* decision and the existing pronouncements by academics and the United States Copyright Office[203] as to the application of the first sale defense to digitally downloaded content, the question should not be regarded as permanently closed. The United States Copyright Office is shortly to embark on a wholesale review of copyright law which will likely include first sale issues amongst a variety of other pressing issues

---

[200] *Id.*

[201] LEAFFER, *supra* note 11, at 329 ("The first sale doctrine can be modified by the parties, but any agreement would be enforced under contract law rather than copyright law").

[202] *Id.*, at 332.

[203] *Id.*, at note 209 ("The tangible nature of a copy is a defining element of the first sale doctrine and is critical to its rationale").

in the digital age.[204] Additionally, questions of exhaustion of digitally transmitted works are arising in other jurisdictions with some surprising results.

For example, some early attempts to create digital versions of "first sale" have succeeded in the European Union.[205] An attempt to create a system to "re-sell" or "re-license" digitally licensed database software was upheld under the first sale doctrine in the European Union Software Directive.[206] The system under consideration in *UsedSoft GmbH v Oracle International Corp*[207] mimicked first sale by ensuring that the original licensee could no longer access the licensed software after transferring it to a third party. The Court of Justice for the European Union (CJEU) limited its decision to the first sale of computer programs under the Software Directive and made no pronouncement on first sale of other forms of digitized copyrighted works, not covered under that Directive. It is unclear to what extent the reasoning in the case interpreting the Software Directive would apply to other copyright works such as books, music and movies. It is also unclear whether digital books, music and movies might be characterized as "software" in their own right and thus be able to take advantage of the CJEU's reasoning in *Oracle*, at least within the European Union.

As with the fair use questions discussed in the previous section, issues about the liability of online intermediaries with respect to facilitating what looks like a "first sale" for the digital age go to the heart of cyberlaw. While these issues should clearly be debated in the context of digital age reviews of copyright law – as will likely be the case in the United States – they should also be central to cyberlaw. As with fair use, the question arises here as to balancing the encouragement of innovations in digital communications technologies with the protection of existing legal rights like intellectual property. While it may be that *ReDigi* is an easy case of copyright piracy described by the defendant as something

---

[204] Statement of Maria A. Pallante, Register of Copyrights, United States Copyright Office before the Subcommittee on Courts, Intellectual Property and the Internet Committee on the Judiciary, United States House of Representatives, 113th Congress, 1st Session, March 20, 2013, The Register's Call for Updates to U.S. Copyright Law, available at http://www.copyright.gov/regstat/2013/regstat03202013.html#_ftn1, last viewed on August 13, 2013.

[205] *UsedSoft GmbH v Oracle International Corp.*, Case C-128/11, 2012 EUR-Lex CE LEX LEXIS (July 3, 2012).

[206] European Union Directive on the Legal protection of computer programs – Marketing of used licences for computer programs downloaded from the internet – Directive 2009/24/EC – Articles 4(2) and 5(1).

[207] Case C-128/11, 2012 EUR-Lex CE LEX LEXIS (July 3, 2012).

else, there will be cases in which an online intermediary is discouraged from engaging in innovation because of concerns about copyright liability. One may even conceptualize *ReDigi* itself as an attempt to create greater consumer choice and competition in downstream markets for digital works.

The main point is not whether *ReDigi* was rightly held liable for copyright infringement, but rather what implications these kinds of fact scenarios hold for the development of online services more generally. While enterprising digital entrepreneurs may proceed to innovate despite perceived risks of copyright infringement – or infringement of other legal rights – a cyberlaw field that more clearly focuses on the nature and contributions of such intermediaries may ultimately give greater *ex ante* guidance to those experimenting with new technological innovations about appropriate boundaries of their legal liability for copyright infringement along with other legal wrongs.

2.4 COPYRIGHT LEGISLATION IN THE DIGITAL AGE

2.4.1 The Digital Millennium Copyright Act

With respect to copyright legislation, this chapter has considered some legislation that has been implemented to regulate intermediated information exchange: for example, the OSCILLA safe harbor provisions for online intermediaries. It has also examined areas where legislation may be a more appropriate solution to particular digital challenges than litigation: for example, a reconceptualization of the first sale doctrine that takes into account the realities of digitally downloaded content. It has not, however, examined all of the legislation that was enacted in the late 1990s in the United States, for example, to cope with perceived challenges of the digital age.

The Digital Millennium Copyright Act (DMCA) contained the OCILLA provisions, but it also did a number of other important – and contentious – things with respect to digital copyright law. It created what might be termed a new "para-copyright" privilege[208] for copyright holders to support technological encryption measures they may attach to

[208] LEAFFER, *supra* note 11, at 404 ("the anti-circumvention provisions of the DMCA may be termed paracopyright in the sense that they strengthen copyright protection by 'regulating conduct which has traditionally fallen outside the regulatory scope of intellectual property law'").

their works to control unauthorized access or use.[209] It also provides some protections to copyright holders who attach copyright management information (CMI) to their digitally distributed works.[210]

While these provisions are undoubtedly relevant to the regulation of digital technology, digital content in general and digital copyrights in particular, they are not necessarily central to the kinds of issues that should properly serve as the focus of a cyberlaw field. To the extent that they may be used as case studies to examine ways in which legislative actions can stifle innovation in online intermediary service markets, they may provide interesting discussion points for those studying cyberlaw. As is the case with telecommunications regulation legislation, these aspects of digital copyright legislation are highly technical and apply in many unexpected ways outside of contexts we might think of as relating to the regulation of intermediated information exchanges.

2.4.2 Anti-Circumvention Provisions

The anti-circumvention provisions of the DMCA, for example, prohibit unauthorized trafficking in a device that can be used to circumvent a copy control measure or trafficking in or using a device that can circumvent an access or copy control measure. The idea is to assist copyright holders to protect against digital pirates who pick digital locks, or assist others to pick digital locks, attached to their works. While in some cases the provisions apply as one might expect – to deter digital piracy – in many cases the provisions have arguably been misused in practice in attempts to extend monopolies in non-copyrighted products or services that incidentally incorporate copyrightable software.[211]

Overall, there is not much litigation involving the anti-circumvention provisions of the DMCA.[212] The litigation there has arisen in varied contexts many of which are not particularly relevant to a discussion of cyberlaw as conceived in this book. For example, manufacturers of garage door openers and computer printers have attempted unsuccessfully

---

[209] 17 U.S.C. § 1201.

[210] 17 U.S.C. § 1202.

[211] See discussion in LEAFFER, *supra* note 11, at 410; Jacqueline Lipton, *The Law of Unintended Consequences: The Digital Millennium Copyright Act and Interoperability*, 62 WASHINGTON & LEE LAW REVIEW 487–546 (2005) [hereinafter, *Unintended Consequences*].

[212] LEAFFER, *supra* note 11, at 410 ("Anticircumvention provisions … have not engendered a vast amount of litigation").

to run DMCA arguments to prevent unauthorized competitors in downstream markets for component parts including garage door "clickers" and printer toner cartridges.[213] The DMCA arguments revolve around the fact that these parts include encrypted software to make them function with the main devices: the garage door openers and computer printers. Because these are not the kinds of situations for which the DMCA was enacted, courts have spent some time attempting to read into the statute ways to avoid such litigation.[214] These are not truly Internet cases other than in the sense that they demonstrate how unfortunately worded cyberspace legislation can have unintended practical consequences outside the cyberlaw field.

Again, these questions are outside the central focus of cyberlaw as conceived here and have more to do with statutory interpretation than the regulation of the balance between existing legal rights and the encouragement of online innovation. Thus, these discussions should not be conceived as something central to cyberlaw even though they relate to legislative attempts to regulate digital technology. The challenges of drafting effective anticircumvention legislation are too technical, and have too much to do with legislative drafting and the policy behind copyright law generally to be of much use in illuminating the questions of balance that should be the main focus of a cyberlaw field.

Some questions about the anti-circumvention provisions do arise in contexts that are more germane to the issues under discussion in this book. For example, case law involving the anti-circumvention provisions of the DMCA has raised significant policy debate about the extent to which the provisions impinge on the fair use defense, and, in turn, on free speech more generally in the digital age.[215] While Congress explicitly provided that nothing in the anticircumvention provisions should be regarded as affecting fair use,[216] or enlarging or diminishing free speech entitlements,[217] the practical impact of the provisions has arguably had some negative effects on downstream users' ability to access works in

---

[213] Lipton, *Unintended Consequences*, *supra* note 211.

[214] LEAFFER, *supra* note 11, at 411.

[215] See discussion in *321 Studios v MGM*, 307 F. Supp.2d 1085, 1099–1103 (2004).

[216] 17 U.S.C. § 1201(c)(1) ("Nothing in this section shall affect rights, remedies, limitations, or defenses to copyright infringement, including fair use, under this title").

[217] 17 U.S.C. § 1201(c)(4) ("Nothing in this section shall enlarge or diminish any rights of free speech or the press for activities using consumer electronics, telecommunications, or computing products").

order to make fair uses of them,[218] and thus arguably stifles free speech.[219] To the extent that these debates revolve around balancing speech against proprietary rights online, they may illuminate more focused discussions on balancing rights of online communications services against existing rights-holders.

2.4.3 Copyright Management Information Provisions

Another set of provisions of the DMCA which is only marginally relevant to the conception of cyberlaw proposed in this book are the provisions that deal with the protection of copyright management information (CMI). For the purposes of the DMCA, CMI is defined as:

> … any of the following information conveyed in connection with copies or phonorecords of a work or performances or displays of a work, including in digital form … :
>
> (1) The title and other information identifying the work, including the information set forth on a notice of copyright.
> (2) The name of, and other identifying information about, the author of a work.
> (3) The name of, and other identifying information about, the copyright owner of the work, including the information set forth in a notice of copyright.
> (4) With the exception of public performances of works by radio and television broadcast stations, the name of, and other identifying information about, a performer whose performance is fixed in a work other than an audiovisual work.
> (5) With the exception of public performances of works by radio and television broadcast stations, in the case of an audiovisual work, the name of, and other identifying information about, a writer, performer, or director who is credited in the audiovisual work.
> (6) Terms and conditions for use of the work.
> (7) Identifying numbers or symbols referring to such information or links to such information.
> (8) Such other information as the Register of Copyrights may prescribe by regulation, except that the Register of Copyrights may not require the provision of any information concerning the user of a copyrighted work.[220]

---

218 See generally discussion in Lipton, *Unintended Consequences*, *supra* note 211.

219 LEAFFER, *supra* note 11, at 409–10.

220 17 U.S.C. § 1202(c).

The CMI provisions of the DMCA create new liability regimes for those who provide or distribute false CMI,[221] or who intentionally remove or alter CMI and distribute the work with the information in its altered form.[222] Even more so than the anti-circumvention provisions, while the CMI provisions are obviously relevant to digital technology regulation and the protection of digital copyrights, they are not central to the themes advanced here as the central tenets of a reconceptualized cyberlaw field. While the ability of copyright holders to obtain greater legal protections for their work in terms of digital notices of ownership and terms of use is significant, these provisions per se do not serve to illuminate the balance between innovations in online communications technologies and digital property rights. The main context in which these provisions would be relevant are in cases where an online intermediary purposely removed or altered CMI and this would be an easy case of an attempt to interfere with the copyright holder's legitimate interests.

2.5 CHAPTER SUMMARY

This chapter has attempted to address the aspects of digital copyright law that exemplify issues germane to the study of cyberlaw reconceptualized as the law of the global intermediated information exchange. As such, it has emphasized some issues that are typically found in existing cyberlaw casebooks, but has also suggested that some digital age challenges for copyright law do not necessarily belong at the central focus of the study of cyberlaw. If cyberlaw appropriately focuses on creating synergies between different fields of law as they relate to the digital exchange of information intermediated by third parties, then copyright questions that focus on the role of such intermediaries should become more central to cyberlaw study. Other copyright questions may be relegated to the background.

Subsequent chapters will demonstrate that by following this pattern with respect to other aspects of digital information law, useful approaches can be developed to cyberlaw as a cohesive body of principles that focuses on achieving a delicate balance between innovations in communications technologies and protection of existing legal rights in information. As noted in the Introduction, much of this debate is really a

[221] 17 U.S.C. § 1202(a).
[222] 17 U.S.C. § 1202(b).

question of balancing access to information against control of information, whether that control be by way of a property right, privacy right or right to protect one's reputation.

The study of cyberlaw itself should be better able than is presently the case to provide guiding principles for online intermediaries whose services may impact the legal rights of others in a variety of contexts including intellectual property, privacy, defamation, and online harassment and bullying. The next chapter remains within the parameters of intellectual property law, contrasting digital trademark issues with digital copyright issues that may be relevant to cyberlaw. Subsequent chapters will then consider how other legal interests play into the paradigm presented here for cyberlaw, focusing respectively on defamation, privacy, and other kinds of potentially damaging online communications.

3. Digital trademark law

3.1 TRADEMARKS IN CYBERSPACE

3.1.1 The Digital Challenges for Trademark Law

Trademarks have proved challenging to online regulation in different ways to copyrights, although again the focus has been on how best to regulate the use of an intangible information product in an intermediated global communications medium. The regulation of trademarks online has impacted different kinds of online intermediaries to the regulation of copyrights, notably the Internet Corporation for Assigned Names and Numbers (ICANN), the body that regulates the Internet domain name system, along with ICANN-approved domain name registrars. As these bodies effectively control the most popular Internet addressing system, they have been at the forefront of attempts to balance various rights and interests in trademarks and brand-names in the online addressing context since the inception of the domain name system.

Internet domain name disputes are in fact a fruitful ground for exploring methods of cyberspace dispute resolution more generally, with reference to the innovative approaches to protecting trademarks in Internet addresses adopted by ICANN under the auspices of the Uniform Domain Name Dispute Resolution Policy (UDRP). More recently, ICANN has developed the Uniform Rapid Suspension System (URS) to be available in disputes involving new generic Top Level Domains (gTLDs) under its recently unveiled new gTLD process.

Search engines, too, have been the subject of concerns about protecting trademarks online. A number of cases have been fought in the United States and other countries involving ways in which search engines utilize trademarks in prioritizing search results and sponsored advertising.[1] Online retailers, including auction sites like eBay, have also been subject to litigation relating to the protection of trademarks in virtual space.[2] All

[1] *Playboy v Netscape*, 354 F.3d 1020 (2004); *Rescuecom v Google*, 562 F.3d 123 (2009).

[2] *Tiffany v eBay*, 600 F.3d 93 (2009).

of these intermediaries serve as the gateways through which brand-name products are accessed and sold online. The attachment of trademark liability to entities such as online retailers, search engines and domain name authorities also raises the issue of primary versus secondary liability for infringement. As we saw in the copyright chapter previously, it is not always an easy matter to ascertain whether online intermediaries are more appropriately held liable as primary infringers or are only potentially liable on a secondary basis for activities engaged in by their customers.

The liability issues play out differently in trademark law than copyright law because of differences in the nature of the two legal fields, and the differing implications of primary versus secondary liability within each field. However, the basic dynamics are very similar: considering the extent to which an entity that enables infringement, but perhaps has no animus to cause infringement, should be held liable. This is a key tenet of the cyberlaw field. One significant benefit of reconceptualizing cyberlaw with more of a focus on the position of intermediaries is that more consistent and unified approaches to questions of primary versus secondary liability online may be developed more generally.

3.1.2 Introduction to Trademarks as Information Products

Like copyrights, trademarks are a form of intangible information-based product. They may be conceived of as "property" or "quasi-property". They are potentially valuable assets of a business that may be transferred between entities, although the legal systems in some jurisdictions – such as federal trademark law in the United States – places restrictions on the kinds of transfers available. For example, in the United States, trademarks may not be sold or licensed separate from the goodwill attached to them.[3]

Trademarks are probably best defined as a means for delineating the goods or services of one enterprise from those of another. Trademark law is justified on a number of policy bases including economic efficiency, decreasing consumer search costs, avoiding fraudulent and deceitful behavior in commerce, and protecting commercial competition.[4] In the United States, the Lanham Act is the federal statute that regulates both registered and unregistered marks. For the purposes of the Lanham Act, "trademark" is defined in the following terms:

---

[3] McCarthy on Trademarks and Unfair Competition, § 18:48 (naked licensing), § 18:23 (sales in gross) (4 ed).

[4] *Id.*, at § 2:1 (underlying policy for trademark law).

> The term "trademark" includes any word, name, symbol, or device, or any combination thereof –
>
> (1) used by a person, or
> (2) which a person has a bona fide intention to use in commerce and applies to register on the principal register established by this chapter, to identify and distinguish his or her goods, including a unique product, from those manufactured or sold by others and to indicate the source of the goods, even if that source is unknown.[5]

The term "service mark" is similarly defined, except with respect to the provision of services rather than goods.[6] These notions of what a trademark is are relatively well harmonized internationally by virtue of treaties such as TRIPs[7] and the Paris Convention.[8] Article 15(1) of TRIPs, for example, sets out the following definition of trademarks and service marks:

> Any sign, or any combination of signs, capable of distinguishing the goods or services of one undertaking from those of other undertakings, shall be capable of constituting a trademark. Such signs, in particular words including personal names, letters, numerals, figurative elements and combinations of colours [sic] as well as any combination of such signs, shall be eligible for registration as trademarks. Where signs are not inherently capable of distinguishing the relevant goods or services, Members may make registrability depend on distinctiveness acquired through use. Members may require, as a condition of registration, that signs be visually perceptible.

As with domestic trademark law in the United States, the underlying idea of a trademark is that it is capable of distinguishing one entity's products or services from those of another. The TRIPs definition also talks about prerequisites for registrability of marks. Most countries protect both registered and unregistered (or common law) marks, but there are several different ways it is done depending on the jurisdiction.

In the United States, for example, the entire federal unfair competition law is more or less encompassed in the Lanham Act. Unregistered marks receive similar protection to registered marks under the statute. By way of contrast, in the United Kingdom unregistered (or common law) marks are protected by tort law related to passing off and other associated torts,

---

[5] 15 U.S.C. § 1127.

[6] *Id.*

[7] The World Trade Organization's Agreement on Trade-Related Aspects of Intellectual Property Rights (TRIPS), negotiated in the 1986–94 Uruguay Round.

[8] Paris Convention for the Protection of Industrial Property (1883).

while only registered marks are protected under the trademarks legislation. Section 2 of the Trade Marks Act of 1994 in the United Kingdom makes this clear:

> (1) A registered trade mark is a property right obtained by the registration of the trade mark under this Act and the proprietor of a registered trade mark has the rights and remedies provided by this Act.
> (2) No proceedings lie to prevent or recover damages for the infringement of an unregistered trade mark as such; but nothing in this Act affects the law relating to passing off.

The British approach differs from the approach in the United States in several ways. For one thing, the legislation in the United Kingdom expressly recognizes a property right in a trademark[9] while the United States' provisions are more equivocal on that score.[10] Additionally, registered and unregistered trademarks are obviously treated under quite separate legal regimes in the United Kingdom as compared with the United States where the entire federal law of trademarks – registered and unregistered – is set out in the Lanham Act. Despite all these differences, the British definition of trademark is very similar to the American definition:

> In this Act a "trade mark" means any sign capable of being represented graphically which is capable of distinguishing goods or services of one undertaking from those of other undertakings.
>
> A trade mark may, in particular, consist of words (including personal names), designs, letters, numerals or the shape of goods or their packaging.[11]

Trademarks have been protected and regulated in a number of ways over the years. However, the basic trademark action has always been trademark infringement which derived originally from the common law of passing off. It is a prohibition on a competitor using a mark in trade or commerce in a manner that could confuse consumers as to the origin of the goods or services.[12]

In more recent years, trademark legislation has broadened to encompass other kinds of trademark-related actions. In the 1980s, many

---

[9] Trade Marks Act (1994), Eng. § 22 ("A registered trade mark is personal property (in Scotland, incorporeal moveable property)").

[10] McCarthy, *supra* note 3, at § 2:14.

[11] Trade Marks Act (1994), Eng. § 1(1).

[12] See, for example, 15 U.S.C. § 1114(1)(a) and 1125(a)(1) (dealing with infringement of registered and unregistered marks respectively).

countries added a dilution action to the trademark legislation. Dilution basically protects "famous" marks[13] against either "blurring" or "tarnishment".[14] The former relates to the creation of sufficient noise around the mark – by using the same or a similar mark on different products – to interfere with the distinctiveness or selling power of the famous mark.[15] The latter relates to using the same or a similar mark on different products in a way that might tarnish the reputation of the famous mark by creating unsavory associations with it.[16] Neither of these cases requires a showing of consumer confusion in the traditional trademark infringement sense, although dilution is often argued alongside infringement on the same facts.

Even more recently, several jurisdictions have included provisions specific to Internet domain names in trademark statutes and other legislation. In 1999, the Lanham Act was amended to include a domestic legal action against "cybersquatting" which in many ways mirrors the provisions of the Uniform Domain Name Dispute Resolution Policy (UDRP) implemented by ICANN around the same time. The American legislation is known as the Anti-Cybersquatting Consumer Protection Act (ACPA). Often, ACPA proceedings are argued alongside infringement and dilution claims where a plaintiff is asserting that the defendant interfered with the plaintiff's trademark in the context of a domain name.

Several state legislatures in the United States have also enacted domain-name-specific regulations that don't necessarily revolve around trademark rights. California has implemented legislation to prevent political cyberfraud,[17] and several states have implemented legislation to protect personal names and prevent other kinds of misleading conduct in the domain space outside of trademark law.[18] On the federal level in the United States, there is also legislation protecting personal names in the domain space outside of trademark law.[19] It is important to remember

---

[13] 15 U.S.C. § 1125(c)(2)(A) (definition of "famous mark").

[14] 15 U.S.C. § 1125(c).

[15] 15 U.S.C. §1125(c)(2)(B)("'dilution by blurring' is association arising from the similarity between a mark or trade name and a famous mark that impairs the distinctiveness of the famous mark").

[16] 15 U.S.C. § 1125(c)(2)(C) ("'dilution by tarnishment' is association arising from the similarity between a mark or trade name and a famous mark that harms the reputation of the famous mark").

[17] CAL. PEN. CODE § 502.

[18] See, for example, discussion in JACQUELINE LIPTON, INTERNET DOMAIN NAMES, TRADEMARKS AND FREE SPEECH, 166–70 (2010) [hereinafter, INTERNET DOMAIN NAMES].

[19] 15 U.S.C. § 8131.

when considering the regulation of the Internet domain space that domain names may coincide with trademarks and raise traditional trademark infringement issues, but many domain name disputes do not involve trademarks, but rather personal names, culturally significant terms or geographical indicators.[20]

Regardless of the complexities of trademark law and the relationship of domain names to trademarks, it should at the very least be obvious that trademarks are pure information products and, as such, have proved problematic on the information superhighway. While trademarks tend to be limited in terms of their geographic reach, domain names and Internet website content is typically accessible globally. Thus, cyberspace breaks down jurisdictional boundaries that have traditionally applied to – and helped with the regulation of – trademarks and service marks in the physical world.

As with other information products, trademarks cannot be utilized online without the involvement of one or more online intermediaries such as Internet service providers, search engines, online retailers and the like. Thus, they raise the issue of intermediary liability when considered in the Internet context. The remainder of this chapter focuses on the ways in which trademark disputes – and associated issues – have arisen online, the kinds of online intermediaries that have been implicated, and the kinds of liabilities that have been attached to these intermediaries. As with the copyright chapter, case studies are presented that emphasize issues common to online intermediaries in an attempt to draw together threads of a more cohesive and unified cyberlaw field.

Like copyrights, trademarks also raise the need to balance free expression against protection of an intellectual property right. However, unlike copyright, the trademark/free speech balance must be struck in a different place. While the value of a copyright is largely in its artistic expression – at least with respect to works at the heart of copyright protection like literature, art and music – the value of a trademark lies in its ability to identify the source of goods or services in commerce. The different functions of these two distinct intellectual property rights has a significant impact on the speech/intellectual property balance. Theoretically, the protection of trademarks should have a much lesser impact on free speech than the protection of copyrights because the trademark right itself does not protect individual expression, but rather is limited to commercial branding.

---

20 LIPTON, INTERNET DOMAIN NAMES, *supra* note 18, at 14–15.

As we saw in the copyright chapter, the regulation and protection of trademarks in cyberspace also implicates a balance between the needs of the trademark holder and the needs of those engaging in technological innovation. The attachment of significant intellectual property burdens on those developing, say, innovative search engine technologies or innovative online retail services could impede the development of those services. Thus, the following discussion focuses heavily not only on balancing intellectual property rights against other competing interests in cyberspace (such as free speech), but importantly on the need to balance those rights against the promotion of new and innovative digital technologies.

3.2 TRADEMARKS AND THE LAW OF THE GLOBAL INTERMEDIATED INFORMATION EXCHANGE

3.2.1 Protecting Trademarks Versus Promoting Technological Innovation

As with the other areas discussed in this text, trademark law raises the challenges inherent in finding a regulatory approach that strikes the appropriate balance between the need to encourage technological innovation and the need to protect existing legal rights. In the context of trademark law, addressing this puzzle has involved the interpretation of both the "commercial use" and "consumer confusion" elements of the infringement action, particularly with respect to the activities of online intermediaries such as search engines and online retailers.

The question of primary versus secondary liability has arisen in the trademark area but hasn't caused as much consternation as in the copyright area, because the nature of a defendant's liability in trademark law isn't as varied as it is in copyright law depending on whether the defendant is considered primarily or secondarily liability for an infringement. As noted in the previous chapter, copyright law involves quite different standards of intent on the defendant's part amongst the different categories of liability. Trademark law does not raise these concerns. In one of the leading American search engine cases, the court, in fact, prevaricated on whether the defendant should be held primarily or secondarily liable for trademark infringement, holding that in the final analysis it made little practical difference.[21]

---

[21] *Playboy v Netscape*, *supra* note 1, at 1024.

While most of the major challenges to trademark law in cyberspace in the domestic context have involved the interpretation and application of the elements of the infringement action, dilution and ACPA proceedings have also raised their own challenges. The ACPA's *in rem* provisions, effectively creating property rights in domain names, have proved interesting in terms of application. However, those issues have become less central to the developing field of cyberlaw in recent years because: (a) most domain name cases are dealt with under the UDRP without the need to resort to the ACPA; and, (b) the apparent home court advantage for American trademark holders in the early days of the ACPA no longer plays out in practice because many domain names are no longer registered in Herndon, Virginia. The ACPA's *in rem* provisions locate the *in rem* action at the place of registration of the domain name,[22] which in the early days of the Internet effectively meant Herndon because Network Solutions was the only registrar and it was located there. Now, the domain name system has been decentralized and even ".com", ".net" and ".org" names are registered all over the world.

The key questions for cyberlaw come back to that balance between technological innovation and intellectual property rights. As search engines, particularly those that make money through keyword advertising, increase in sophistication, more and more subtle uses of trademarks to generate advertisements for competitors are developed. The extent to which this should be regarded as an infringement of trademark law has plagued courts the world over, and a number of leading cases are discussed below. Trademarks have also raised challenges for retailers and other online services that engage in a variety of activities, such as providing resale markets for used goods or providing forums for customers to comment on goods. These are activities that presumably regulators want to encourage. However, to the extent that trademarks are used without authorization – particularly in cases where they are attached to counterfeit goods – the question arises as to whether the online services facilitating the transactions should be held liable. This has been an issue for eBay in recent years. While eBay has a number of procedures and policies in place to deter the sale of counterfeit goods over its website, there is only so much it can do before the risks and associated costs of infringement actions threaten its business model.

Search engines have also faced trademark liability for various technological innovations involving their search algorithms' ability to index websites based on things like metatags and web content that may be

---

[22] 15 U.S.C. § 1125(d)(2).

misleading. For example, if a competitor of Nike uses the Nike trademark in a metatag for its website or has text on the website that includes the "Nike" mark, to what extent should the search engine be liable for prioritizing the competitor's website in search results when the Internet user is searching for Nike?

Other than the questions raised by trademark legislation for application in cyberspace, trademark law is also instructive in terms of regulating the Internet domain name space because alternate regulatory approaches have developed involving ICANN and its authorized registries to protect trademarks in the domain space. In the early days of the Internet, courts were faced with the potential liability of domain name registries for registering domain names that corresponded with others' trademarks. While those questions have largely been resolved in practice by the implementation of the UDRP, the new gTLD process unveiled by ICANN raises a whole host of new issues as more and more generic Top Level Domains come into play.[23]

3.2.2 Primary Versus Secondary Liability Questions for Trademark Law Online

As noted in the previous sub-section, trademark law stands in sharp contrast to copyright law in terms of questions about the extent to which an online intermediary might be primarily versus secondarily liable for infringements involving another party. In the American case of *Playboy v Netscape*, the Ninth Circuit held that it was irrelevant whether the defendant search engine was regarded as being potentially primarily or secondarily liability for infringement because that question would not affect the liability determination overall.[24] The facts of the case were a little different to those involving search engines in the copyright context.

Trademark cases in the search engine context tend to involve the potential liability for selling trademarked keywords for Internet advertising schemes. These terms are generally sold to competitors of the mark holders to enable competitors' marks to be prioritized in search results when an Internet user searches for the trademarked term. Primary liability for search engines is possible in the trademark context in cases

---

[23] See, for example, discussion in Mary Wong and Jacqueline Lipton, *Imperatives of Private Arbitration in International Intellectual Property Disputes*, 24 SINGAPORE ACADEMY OF LAW JOURNAL 978 (2012); Jacqueline Lipton and Mary Wong, *Trademarks and Free Speech in ICANN's new gTLD Process*, 38 MONASH LAW REVIEW 188 (2012).

[24] *Playboy v Netscape*, *supra* note 1, at 1024.

where the search engines themselves commercially transact in others' marks in this way.

There may be trademark defenses available to search engines in these kinds of cases. However, to date, in the United States at least, the trademark defenses have not played a key role in determining infringement in the search engine context. In *Playboy v Netscape*, the court considered the availability of the fair use defense to the search engine's activities, ultimately holding that the defendant's activities could not be excused as a fair use.[25]

The *Netscape* case was limited by agreement between the parties to questions involving misleadingly labeled advertisements that arose in search engine results. In her concurrence, Judge Berzon was careful to emphasize this point, saying: "I do not think it is reasonable to find initial interest confusion when a consumer is never confused as to source or affiliation, but instead knows, or should know, from the outset that a product or web link is not related to that of the trademark holder because the list produced by the search engine so informs him".[26] In this passage, Judge Berzon was not specifically referring to the application of the fair use defense, but rather suggesting at the outset that the action for infringement would not lie in the absence of consumer confusion.

It is likely that fair use is less relevant to cyberlaw questions concerning trademark infringement than those involving copyright infringement. In the trademark context, much of what could be considered fair use on the defendant's part could equally be considered a failure of the plaintiff to make out the consumer confusion requirement. Courts in trademark cases often err on the side of spending more time on the consumer confusion aspect of infringement – with the burden on the plaintiff to establish confusion – than on the fair use defense – with the associated burden on the defendant.

Outside of the search engine context, the question of primary versus secondary liability of online intermediaries has arisen in the online resellers' market, notably in the case of *Tiffany v eBay*[27] which is discussed below. But again the outcome of the case did not hinge on the distinction between primary and secondary liability. In that case, online

---

[25] *Id.*, at 1029 ("Because we have found that a genuine issue of fact exists as to likelihood of confusion … , we must deny summary judgment as to the fair use defense. A fair use may not be a confusing use").

[26] *Id.*, at 1034–35.

[27] See *supra* note 2.

auction service eBay was held to be neither directly nor contributorily liable for infringements by third party customers of Tiffany's marks.[28]

Before considering this case, it is worth completing a discussion of search engine liability by noting that courts have also considered the role of competitors of trademark holder plaintiffs as defendants in search engine cases, thereby more squarely raising the prospect of direct liability. Where a competitor of a trademark holder actively purchases the trademark to key its own advertisements in an Internet search, that competitor may be regarded as more squarely involved in a primary infringement than perhaps the search engine itself, even though the search engine may actively sell the term to the competitor.

The British case of *Interflora v Marks and Spencer*[29] is an example of an action by a trademark holder against a competitor with respect to the competitor's use of its trademark for keyword advertising purposes. Interflora is a global provider of flower delivery services. Marks and Spencer provides competing services within the United Kingdom. Marks and Spencer had utilized the Interflora mark in the search engine context to have its services show up as sponsored advertisements in search engine results when Internet users searched for Interflora. The British courts were not convinced that reasonably careful Internet users would realize, on seeing the sponsored advertisements, that Marks and Spencer was not connected with the Interflora network, thus potentially causing consumer confusion. Thus, Marks and Spencer was held liable for trademark infringement as a primary infringer.[30]

Returning to the question of online reseller liability for trademark infringement – and the *eBay* litigation – it is worth noting that auction sites like eBay have a different relationship to trademark infringement than search engines. Online auction houses provide a forum for the resale of trademarked goods, but unlike the keyword advertising context they do not actively sell the marks themselves. Their profit margins come from the fees paid through use of their services, not through suggesting and selling terms – sometimes trademarked terms – which their customers may want to use for targeted advertising purposes. Because services like eBay seem, at least on their face, to be less actively involved in specific uses of given trademarks, it might seem reasonable to think that as a matter of policy they should face less trademark liability than search engines that directly profit from sale of trademarked terms to competitors

---

28 *Id.*

29 *Interflora v Marks & Spencer* [2013] EWHC 273 (Ch).

30 *Id.*, at para. 326.

of the markholders. At the very least, one might think that plaintiffs seeking to protect marks against the activities of online auction services should face a higher burden to establish liability.

Another way of considering the distinction between search engines and online auction houses as intermediaries dealing with trademarked terms is to look at the underlying policy balance between the protection of trademarks and the promotion of technologically innovative services. While this exercise undoubtedly involves making value judgments on a case-by-case basis, one might say that a search engine's key innovations are outside the scope of keyword advertising, and that the advertising is simply one financial model to help it finance its online activities. On the other hand, an online auction site's major online activities involve sales of brand-name products and, provided that it has reasonable measures in place to prevent trademark infringement, the law should encourage its primary activities.

This distinction really revolves around the premise that the law should protect the major innovative contributions of online services, rather than secondary means for financing those activities. Of course those two questions can be difficult to separate in practice. How can an intermediary innovate without a workable financial model? Nevertheless, it might be reasonable for regulators to assume that workable financial models should not rely on the infringement of existing property rights.

In the *eBay* case, the plaintiff had argued that eBay should be held directly and indirectly liable for infringements of its marks with respect to counterfeit goods available via the eBay website. While eBay had implemented a number of anti-fraud measures, it also promoted the sale of premium-brand jewelry over its website in various ways including hyperlinking to brand-name merchandise, and purchasing sponsored link advertisements in search engines to promote the availability of brand-name jewelry (including Tiffany jewelry) on its website. Both the district court and the appeal court rejected Tiffany's arguments that eBay should be held directly or secondarily liable for trademark infringement, although the case was remanded on a separate false advertising claim.

Unlike *Playboy v Netscape*, the Second Circuit Court of Appeals in *eBay* took more time to distinguish between questions of primary versus secondary liability for trademark infringement in the online auction site context. On the question of direct infringement, the court held that there cannot be liability in circumstances where a defendant simply used the plaintiff's marks to accurately describe the nature of the genuine goods offered for sale on its website without suggesting any actual affiliation or sponsorship between the plaintiff and the defendant.[31]

The court prevaricated on the question whether a defendant's use of a plaintiff's mark to describe genuine goods was rightly considered a part of the fair use defense – or more specifically nominative use[32] – or was rather an element of the action itself. One of the reasons why the court seemed disinclined to rule on the nature and applicability of the nominative use defense was that while nominative use had been accepted in other circuits, the second circuit had never expressly adopted or rejected the doctrine at the time of the litigation.[33] The court avoided the need to address whether nominative use should be adopted in the second circuit, and preferred to resolve the case by simply saying that a defendant's use of a mark is not unlawful where it is used to describe genuine goods of the plaintiff.[34]

With respect to Tiffany's argument that eBay knew, or should have known, about the counterfeit goods sold over its website, the Second Circuit Court of Appeals felt that it was important to relegate that discussion to an examination of eBay's potential *contributory* liability.[35] The court did not want to muddy the waters of direct liability for infringement with arguments about knowledge of others' infringements. The court was mindful of the need to separate questions of direct liability

---

31 *Tiffany v eBay*, *supra* note 2, at 103 ("eBay's use of Tiffany's mark on its website and in sponsored links was lawful. eBay used the mark to describe accurately the genuine Tiffany goods offered for sale on its website. And none of eBay's uses of the mark suggested that Tiffany affiliated itself with eBay or endorsed the sale of its products through eBay's website").

32 *Id.*, at 102–3.

33 *Id.*, at 102 ("We have referred to the [nominative use] doctrine, albeit without adopting or rejected it … . Other circuits have done similarly").

34 *Id.*, at 102–3 ("We need not address the viability of the [nominative use] doctrine to resolve Tiffany's claim, however. We have recognized that a defendant may not lawfully use a plaintiff's trademark where doing so is necessary to describe the plaintiff's product and does not imply a false affiliation or endorsement by the plaintiff of the defendant").

35 *Id.*, at 103 ("Tiffany argues … that even if eBay had the right to use its mark with respect to the resale of genuine Tiffany merchandise, eBay infringed the mark because it knew or had reason to know that there was 'a substantial problem with the sale of counterfeit [Tiffany] silver jewelry' on the eBay website … . eBay's knowledge *vel non* that counterfeit Tiffany wares were offered through its website is relevant to the issue of whether eBay contributed to the direct infringement of Tiffany's mark by the counterfeiting vendors themselves, or whether eBay bears liability for false advertising. But it is not a basis for a claim of direct trademark infringement against eBay …").

from questions that arise when a defendant may have been in some way involved in infringing conduct by others. This is very often the case with online intermediaries – that they do not generate infringements themselves, but facilitate infringements by others. Thus the court's decision to separate the direct and indirect liability questions is instructive for the purposes of this discussion.

While many of the copyright cases have dealt with separating direct and indirect liability in cyberspace, trademark law has historically not spent as much time developing secondary liability doctrines.[36] In particular, as noted by the *eBay* court, judges have not spent much time applying trademark law's secondary liability doctrines in cyberspace and, as a result, they are somewhat under-conceptualized.[37] A reformulated cyberlaw field that focuses on the primary versus secondary liability issues of online intermediaries would benefit greatly from a more detailed development of secondary liability in trademark law. Additionally, the field of cyberlaw is an excellent forum within which to consider these questions, as it gives scholars and others the benefit of contrasting secondary liability for trademark infringement in cyberspace with secondary liability for infringements of other legal rights online.

The second circuit's examination of contributory trademark infringement is instructive for the development of intermediary liability principles more generally as it draws from first principles of secondary liability[38] in much the same way the Supreme Court of the United States did in the copyright context in *Grokster*.[39] While there were few to no cyberspace cases of contributory trademark infringement at the time of the *eBay* decision, the court went back to cases of contributory infringement in the physical world, notably the Supreme Court's decision in *Inwood Laboratories v Ives Laboratories*.[40] The *eBay* court noted that the problem with the Supreme Court precedent, when considering its application to cyberspace intermediaries, is that *Inwood* as well as most other pre-Internet cases dealt with infringement actions against manufacturers

---

[36] *Id.*

[37] *Id.*, at 105 ("The limited case law leaves the law of contributory trademark infringement ill-defined. Although we are not the first court to consider the application of [the doctrine] to the Internet, … we are apparently the first to consider its application to the online marketplace").

[38] *Id.*, at 103 ("Contributory trademark infringement is a judicially created doctrine that derives from the common law of torts").

[39] See discussion in Part 2.3.4, *supra.*

[40] 456 U.S. 844 (1982).

and distributors of goods rather than those providing services.[41] However, the court did identify some service providers in the physical world, such as flea markets, that had run afoul of the doctrine in cases where that defendant "exercises sufficient control over the infringing conduct".[42]

The court then noted the paucity of cyberspace cases raising indirect trademark infringement issues, and identifying one other online contributory infringement case: *Lockheed Martin v Network Solutions*.[43] That case was not particularly helpful to the discussion in *eBay* because it concerned the potential liability of Network Solutions as a domain name registrar for the registration of a domain name that corresponded with the plaintiff's marks. While it was a case of a potential contribution by the defendant to the trademark infringing activities of a third party, the context was very different. In any event, the domain name registrar issues were soon resolved by the adoption of the UDRP which is discussed later in this chapter. Courts did absolve Network Solutions in early decisions for secondary liability for trademark infringement. Courts were generally mindful of the costs that would be imposed on that special class of intermediaries if they were required to undertake trademark due diligence on a global scale before registering any given domain name.[44]

The imposition of such obligations would have significantly chilled the development of the domain name system at a time when it was first gaining ground. At the end of the day it proved more workable and cost-effective for ICANN to implement the UDRP which placed the burden on a domain name registrant to represent and warrant to the registering authority that she was not infringing anyone else's rights by applying for a given domain name.[45]

---

41 *Tiffany v eBay*, *supra* note 2, at 104 ("*Inwood's* test for contributory trademark infringement applies on its face to manufacturers and distributors of goods").

42 *Id.*

43 194 F.3d 980 (9th Cir. 1999).

44 See, for example, *Lockheed Martin v Network Solutions*, 194 F.3d 980 (9th Cir. 1999).

45 UDRP, cl. 2 ("By applying to register a domain name, or by asking us to maintain or renew a domain name registration, you hereby represent and warrant to us that: (a) the statements that you made in your Registration Agreement are complete and accurate; (b) to your knowledge, the registration of the domain name will not infringe upon or otherwise violate the rights of any third party; (c) you are not registering the domain name for an unlawful purpose; and (d) you will not knowingly use the domain name in violation of any applicable laws or regulations. It is your responsibility to determine whether your domain name registration infringes or violates someone else's rights").

The second circuit in *eBay* identified two ways in which a service provider might be contributorily liable for the infringing conduct of third parties: (1) if the service provider intentionally induces the third parties to infringe the mark; or (2) if it continues providing services to a third party with knowledge, or with reason to know, that the third party is engaging in trademark infringement.[46] On the facts, the court was not convinced that the first scenario was made out, so it focused on the second. It held that eBay was not liable on this basis by distinguishing between eBay's general knowledge about counterfeiting on its website and the kind of specific knowledge it would have to have had to support a contributory infringement claim:

> [W]e agree with the district court that "Tiffany's general allegations of counterfeiting failed to provide eBay with the knowledge required under *Inwood*. Tiffany's demand letters … did not identify particular sellers who Tiffany thought were then offering or would offer counterfeit goods. And although … buyer complaints gave eBay reason to know that certain sellers had been selling counterfeits, those sellers' listings were removed and repeat offenders were suspended from the eBay site. Thus Tiffany failed to demonstrate that eBay was supplying its service to individuals who knew or had reason to know were selling counterfeit Tiffany goods.[47] [citations omitted]

Interestingly, because of the dearth of litigation on contributory trademark infringement, the court in *eBay* looked to copyright law for guidance on the secondary liability principles.[48] It spent some time discussing the development and application of the contributory liability doctrine in copyright law in *Sony v Universal*.[49] That case, in turn, had discussed the development of the contributory liability doctrine in patent law.[50] Indeed, the Supreme Court in *Sony* expressly borrowed the patent doctrine and consciously applied it to copyright law.[51]

The fact that courts have borrowed ideas from other areas of law in developing secondary liability doctrines emphasizes the desirability of creating forums within which such doctrines can be considered across various areas of law. A reconceptualized cyberlaw that focuses on the role of intermediaries automatically creates a theoretical space within which to debate secondary liability doctrines across various fields of law,

---

[46] *Tiffany v eBay*, *supra* note 2, at 105.
[47] *Id.*, at 109.
[48] *Id.*
[49] 464 U.S. 417 (1984).
[50] *Id.*, at 434–42.
[51] *Id.*

thus potentially resulting in more cohesive and unified approaches to these liability issues, as well as to the distinction between primary and secondary liability.

3.2.3 Trademark Law's Commercial Use Requirement

Another pressure point for trademark law in the digital age that has played out in the courts in many different countries is the "in commerce" or "commercial use" requirement for infringement and dilution actions. This requirement is variously stated in the laws of different countries and has been variously interpreted by courts depending on the wording of the relevant jurisdiction's statute and the constitutional bases for the requirement. In the United States in particular, trademark law's commercial use requirement is important because the entire federal trademark statute is premised on the commerce clause of the United States Constitution.[52]

While laws in a number of European Union Member States may set out their own take on the "in commerce" requirement for trademark infringement and dilution actions, the European Union Trademark Directive conceptualizes the requirement, in the infringement context at least, in terms of a use by the defendant of the plaintiff's mark or a similar mark "in the course of trade".[53] This wording is mirrored in the infringement action under the British domestic trademark legislation.[54]

While the interpretation of trademark law's commercial use requirement may at first sound arcane and not particularly relevant to cyberlaw, debates about what the concept means have been central to questions of intermediary liability for trademark infringement online. Infringement was initially developed to prevent uses of marks by competitors that might confuse consumers as to the source of products or services. Thus, the kinds of uses made by defendants were typically trademark-like uses: that is to say, affixing the plaintiff's mark on similar goods manufactured and distributed by the defendant. For example, selling a pair of sneakers made by a competitor of Nike with a Nike "swoosh" logo prominently affixed.

---

52 See *U.S. v Moghadan*, 175 F.3d 1269, para. III (1999); *Playboy v Netscape*, *supra* note 1, at 144–45.

53 First Council Directive 89/104/EEC of 21 December 1988 to approximate the laws of the Member States relating to trade marks; available at http://eur-lex.europa.eu/LexUriServ/LexUriServ.do?uri=CELEX:31989L0104:en:HTML, last viewed on June 23, 2014; art. 5.

54 Trade Marks Act (1994), Eng., § 10.

The digital age puts new pressure on the commercial use requirement in the sense that many of the uses made by Internet intermediary defendants do not fit the typical mold. The sale of trademarks as keyword search terms by Internet search engines is an obvious example. While this use is commercial in the sense that the defendant search engine receives a financial gain from the sale of the keywords, it is not the traditional type of use with which trademark law has concerned itself. Thus, courts have had to struggle with the extent to which trademark infringement actions require the defendant to make a trademark-like use of the plaintiff's term or whether any form of commercial use will suffice. The answer to the question may depend, to a significant extent, on the wording of the relevant legislation. However, most jurisdictions – as noted above – word their statutes in fairly broad terms relating to "commercial use" or "use in the course of trade" which at least facially may be broad enough to cover uses outside the traditional infringement paradigm.

Outside doctrinal questions regarding the interpretation of trademark statutes lie the policy questions about balancing technological innovation against intellectual property rights. The broader the approach courts take to interpreting the commercial use requirement, the more potential risk of liability is thrust on online intermediaries seeking to innovate in cyberspace. However, if courts interpret the concept narrowly to encompass only traditional trademark uses by intermediary defendants, trademark holders' property rights may not be sufficiently protected in online marketplaces.

Naturally, the interpretation of the commercial use requirement is not the final step in the balance between technological innovation and the protection of property rights in cyberspace. Trademark infringement actions also require a showing of likelihood of consumer confusion. It may be that the consumer confusion element of the action is the more appropriate place to engage in the policy battle to balance these interests in cyberspace. An emphasis on consumer confusion in this context might be supported on the basis that consumer confusion is really the mainstay of the infringement action and is perhaps a more important element for courts to focus on in the digital age to strike the appropriate policy balance.

While most conduct on the Internet can be – and indeed has been – characterized as "commercial",[55] it may be that the commercial use

---

[55] See, for example, *Planned Parenthood Federation of America v Bucci*, 42 U.S.P.Q. 1430 (S.D.N.Y. 1999), para. 4.

aspect of trademark law really does not have much work to do in cyberspace. It has not been difficult for courts to decide that most online activities can be characterized as commercial in some sense. If this continues to be the prevailing view, the commercial use requirement in trademark law will remain ill-equipped as a policy forum within which to balance the needs of online innovators against the rights of trademark holders.

However, some Internet cases have analyzed the extent to which online intermediaries' uses of plaintiffs' trademarks may be said to be commercial uses for the purposes of trademark law. These cases are worth discussing, particularly in the context of a larger argument about reframing the cyberlaw debate to focus more on the balance of competing rights and interests in online commerce and communication. It may be that the commercial use requirement in trademark law should be given more work to do in future cases. The developing area of cyberlaw, with a focus on the role of online intermediaries, may be the place to advance some arguments in favor of this view. Another advantage of reconsidering the commercial use aspect of the defendants' conduct in the case of online intermediaries is that *dilution* actions also require a commercial use by the defendant of the plaintiff's mark, and there is no consumer confusion element present in the dilution action. Thus the application of trademark dilution law in cyberspace cannot benefit from a focus on consumer confusion.

Several American cases have considered the application of trademark law's commercial use requirement in the context of online intermediaries. The results of the cases have been context-dependent focusing on the case-by-case operation of the technology in question in a given situation. For example, in *1-800 Contacts v WhenU.com*,[56] the Second Circuit considered a technology involving "pop-up ad" technology. In this case, the defendant had used the plaintiff's marks in internal directories which it used to key pop-up ads to Internet users' computer screens depending on what they were searching for. For example, if an Internet user searched for "eye care", an advertisement for an optometrist may pop up on her screen. Unlike the defendant in *Playboy v Netscape*, the defendant in *1-800 Contacts* did not sell keywords. It simply took money for keying ads to relevant search terms. The trademarks used by the defendant were used internally within its software.

Holding that this kind of use did not amount to a commercial use in the trademark context, the court noted that:

---

[56] 414 F.3d 400 (2005).

> A company's internal utilization of a trademark in a way that does not communicate it to the public is analogous to an individual's private thoughts about a trademark. Such conduct simply does not violate the Lanham Act, which is concerned with the use of trademarks in connection with the sale of goods or services in a manner likely to lead to consumer confusion as to the source of such goods or services.[57]

Here, the court contemplates that in order to be a commercial use for trademark purposes, the defendant must not only communicate the mark to someone else, but that it must communicate the mark *in connection with the sale of goods or services*. This raises the question as to whether a defendant search engine that actually *sells* trademarked terms to advertisers in competition with the mark holders would satisfy the commercial use requirement.

That question was answered in the affirmative by the Second Circuit in 2000 in a consideration of Google's keyword advertising service in the case of *Rescuecom v Google*.[58] As with the search engine in *Playboy v Netscape*, Google was selling keywords to competitors of mark holders to trigger sponsored ad results to Internet user searches. Google relied on the precedent in *1-800 Contacts*, arguing that its use of the trademarked terms was not in commerce for the purposes of trademark law, but was rather an internal use by its software. The court, however, distinguished the earlier case on the basis that in *1-800 Contacts*, the display of a competitor's pop-up advertisement was not based on anything the defendant did in recommending or selling any particular trademark to a third party.[59] In *Rescuecom*, however, Google not only sold the Rescuecom mark to Rescuecom's competitors in its keyword advertising scheme, but also encouraged the purchase of the mark by competitors through its "Keyword Suggestion Tool".[60] According to the court, these uses could not be described as mere internal uses and were rather commercial uses as contemplated by the Lanham Act.

The *Rescuecom* court was mindful of the role played by search engines in cyberspace and expressly considered the balance between innovations in search engine technologies against the rights of trademark holders. The court distinguished *1-800 Contacts* to ensure that technological innovations that internally required use of trademarks would not run afoul of trademark infringement law, while commercial activities regarded as

[57] *Id.*, at 409.
[58] *Rescuecom v Google*, *supra* note 1.
[59] *Id.*, at 125–26.
[60] *Id.*

potentially taking unfair advantage of a plaintiff's mark would not be insulated from liability. The court also emphasized that the commercial use enquiry would not be the end of the question and that search engines would only be liable for their commercial activities involving trademarks if those activities caused consumer confusion:

> We did not imply in *1-800* that an alleged infringer's use of a trademark in an internal software program insulates the alleged infringer from a charge of infringement, no matter how likely the use is to cause confusion in the marketplace. If we were to adopt Google['s] argument, the operators of search engines would be free to use trademarks in ways designed to deceive and cause consumer confusion. This is surely neither within the intention nor the letter of the Lanham Act.[61]

The court's approach here is a good example of the tendency by American courts to err on the side of placing a focus on the consumer confusion aspects of infringement rather than the commercial use aspects in deciding the liability of online intermediaries. That may indeed be a sensible approach in practice, given the purposes of trademark infringement law. However, it will not assist with application of trademark dilution law to the Internet. And an approach to infringement that is overly focused on the consumer confusion requirement to the detriment of considering the commercial use requirement may lead to missed opportunities in developing coherent policies for intermediary liability in cyberspace. Perhaps courts could change their approach to discuss consumer confusion issues *before* commercial use issues in American infringement litigation. That way, if there is no consumer confusion, the court would not have to concern itself with the commercial use requirement at all. The requirement need only be addressed if a likelihood of consumer confusion is made out on the facts of the case.

It is perhaps worth noting that the Court of Justice for the European Union (CJEU) has taken a fairly broad interpretation of the "use in the course of trade" requirement in the European Union Trademark Directive, at least in the context of competitors using a plaintiff's marks. In this context, European courts would have to spend more time addressing the other aspects of an infringement proceeding. In *Interflora v Marks and Spencer*,[62] for example, the court held that keyword advertising uses of a trademarked term by a competitor of the mark holder would satisfy the

---

61 *Id.*, at 130.

62 *Interflora v Marks & Spencer*, [2012] FSR 3.

"use in the course of trade" requirement,[63] but that it was important for the court to focus on the other aspects of a trademark infringement claim before making a final determination on the issue.[64]

However, the CJEU has taken a different tack on the question whether a search engine's keyword advertising activities satisfy the trade use requirements of the Directive. The court examined Google's keyword advertising program in *Google France v Louis Vuitton*.[65] It noted the general principle for interpreting the "use in the course of trade" language from the Trademark Directive as follows: "The use of a sign identical with a trade mark [sic] constitutes use in the course of trade where it occurs in the context of commercial activity with a view to economic advantage and not as a private matter …".[66]

The court went on to hold that while the advertisers competing with the trademark holder were using the plaintiffs' marks "in the context of a commercial activity",[67] that was not necessarily the case with respect to the search engine's use of the marks. While Google may have operated "in the course of trade" in terms of its keyword advertising program,[68] it was not clear to the court that Google had necessarily "used" the marks in the sense contemplated by the Directive.[69] According to the court, Google did not engage in a prohibited use even though it was paid by its customers for its keyword advertising services: "The fact of creating the technical conditions necessary for the use of a sign and being paid for

---

63 *Id.*, at para. 30.

64 *Id.*, at para. 31 ("Nevertheless, the proprietor of the trade mark cannot prevent the use of a sign identical to its trade mark as a keyword unless all the conditions provided for to that end in Article 5 of Directive 89/104 and Article 9 of Regulation No 40/94 and by the case-law relating thereto are met").

65 Joined Cases C-236/08 to C-238/08, March 23, 2010 (available at: http://curia.europa.eu/juris/liste.jsf?num=C-236/08#, last viewed on June 23, 2014).

66 *Id.*, at para. 50.

67 *Id.*, at para. 52 ("From the advertiser's point of view, the selection of a keyword identical with a trade mark has the object and effect of displaying an advertising link to the site on which he offers his goods and services for sale. Since the sign selected as a keyword is the means used to trigger that ad display, it cannot be disputed that the advertiser indeed uses it in the context of commercial activity and not as a private matter").

68 *Id.*, at para. 55 ("[Google] operates 'in the course of trade' when it permits advertisers to select, as keywords, signs identical with trade marks, stores those signs and displays its clients' ads on the basis thereof, it does not follow, however, from those factors that that service provider itself 'uses' those signs within the terms of [the Directive]").

69 *Id.*

that service does not mean that the party offering the service itself uses the sign".[70]

Thus, we are seeing a divergence in approach with respect to the commercial use requirement of trademark infringement between the European Union and the United States. This may be attributed in part to the different wording in the legislation, although the CJEU focused on the "use" language rather than the "commerce/trade" language and the latter is the key respect in which the legislative approaches differ. One might criticize the CJEU's approach for divorcing the "use" aspect of the requirement from the "trade" aspect. It is arguable that "use in the course of trade" should be interpreted as one unified concept and that the court's separation of the two concepts is an artificial and illogical construct.

In some ways it seems that the *Google France* court was more concerned with setting policy than in interpreting the provisions of the Directive. One could explain the decision by saying that the court was mindful of the balance that forms the basis of the discussion in this book: that between promoting technological innovation while protecting existing legal rights, in this case, trademark rights. The court may have felt that trademark rights could be sufficiently protected in practice by imposing liability on competitors who purchase keywords, and extending some protection to search engines to encourage the provision and development of their innovative services.

Of course, Google was receiving financial gain to support its service through keyword advertising and it is possible to argue, as suggested in the previous discussion, that technological innovation should not be encouraged to the extent that its financing relies on infringement of existing legal rights. However, to the extent that Google needs to resort to programs like keyword advertising to finance its innovative activities – the provision of increasingly sophisticated search engines and associated services – the CJEU's approach may have some merit.

A comparison of the European and American approaches to search engine liability under the "use" aspect of trademark infringement law supports the need to develop a theoretical space in which online intermediary liability questions can be discussed comprehensively, and on a global scale. The nature of intermediary liability raises similar issues across different jurisdictions. Considering such liability as part of a more targeted study of cyberlaw allows synergies to be developed across jurisdictions and across disparate fields of law.

---

[70] *Id.*, at para. 57.

3.2.4 Trademark Infringement and Consumer Confusion

Another issue that has proved an interesting area for analysis in the cyber-trademark arena is the consumer confusion element of the infringement action. As noted in previous sections, consumer confusion is the mainstay of the infringement action, so much so that American courts are willing to fairly readily find the "commercial use" requirement made out in the case of online intermediaries so the analysis can focus on confusion. There are good reasons for infringement cases – particularly those that arise in new cyberspace contexts – to focus on confusion even to the detriment of a detailed analysis of the commercial use requirement. After all, the point of infringement is to prevent consumers being misled as to the source of products or services. To the extent that an online intermediary's activities result in such confusion, they should be prohibited or at least closely monitored to ensure an optimal balance between their own innovations/contributions in cyberspace and the need to protect trademark holders' rights.

However, it should not be forgotten that trademark law requires some link between commercial use and consumer confusion as a policy matter. As the CJEU pointed out in the *Google France* litigation, not all uses that take place in the course of trade are "uses" within the meaning of the requirement in the Trademark Directive. Even if consumers may ultimately be confused by an online activity in which an intermediary took part, if that intermediary's activities were not the kind of conduct trademark law has historically prevented, the courts should examine the facts carefully to ensure liability questions are appropriately decided. In other words, while trademark law needs to adapt to new online contexts, and the prevention of consumer confusion may be the mainstay of the infringement inquiry, liability should not be too readily attached to intermediaries that provide valuable innovative online services.

Consumer confusion can be a difficult element of the infringement action to apply in practice. While the trademark legislation prohibits conduct which is likely to cause confusion as to the source of goods or services,[71] there is no statutory definition of the term. Rather, courts have developed common law tests for consumer confusion which vary from circuit to circuit in the United States – although the key elements are fairly similar. Like the fair use defense in copyright law, the consumer confusion principles in trademark law are flexibly applied by courts.

[71] McCarthy, *supra* note 3, at § 2:8 ("the keystone of that portion of unfair competition law which relates to trademarks is the avoidance of a likelihood of confusion in the minds of the buying public").

Each circuit court has developed a set of "likelihood of confusion" factors[72] but, as with the four fair use factors in copyright law, some may receive greater or lesser prominence depending on the facts of a given case.[73] Additionally, the test is not an exclusive test. Courts are permitted to take other issues into account in determining likelihood of confusion.[74]

One of the challenges raised by the Internet for the consumer confusion test is, in fact, in the specifics of applying the likelihood of confusion factors in cyberspace. Some of the factors – such as marketing channels used by the respective parties – arguably are much less relevant in virtual space than in the real world. For example, one could easily analyze a real world case where one party advertised through a national television campaign and the other advertised in a local newssheet as being a case where the parties utilized different marketing channels. In that case, the marketing channels factor would weigh against the plaintiff. The less aligned the marketing channels, the less consumers would be likely to be confused – because different groups of consumers would be exposed to the different marketing channels. However, on the Internet, things are a little different because of its global reach.

As Judge Nelson opined in *Playboy v Netscape* when considering the application of the marketing channels factor to the facts at hand:

> This factor is equivocal. [The plaintiff] and the advertisers use identical marketing channels: the Internet. More specifically, each of their sites appears on defendants' search results pages. Given the broad use of the Internet today, the same could be said for countless companies. Thus, this factor merits little weight.[75]

Other courts facing the applicability of the marketing channels factor in Internet cases have been equally unconvinced of its continued relevance. In *Bally v Faber*, a case that did not involve an online intermediary, the court was faced with problems raised by an Internet gripesite that criticized, and made fun of, the products and services offered by the plaintiff.[76] The plaintiff had proceeded against the gripesite operator on a number of legal grounds, including trademark infringement and dilution, and was unsuccessful on all counts.

For the purposes of this discussion, Bally's arguments on infringement with respect to the "marketing channels used" factor is instructive of the

---

72 *Id.*, at § 23:19.

73 *Id.*

74 *Id.*

75 *Playboy v Netscape*, *supra* note 1, at 1028.

76 29 F. Supp.2d 1161 (C.D. Cal 1998).

larger point that this factor is increasingly irrelevant online. Bally had argued that this factor weighed in favor of infringement because both parties used the same marketing channel – the Internet. The court was not persuaded and ultimately held that the marketing channels factor was neutral at best and likely cuts against Bally because the parties' goods and services were unrelated.[77] Bally provided fitness services while the defendant provided consumer commentary. This is an interesting approach because it really sidesteps the issue of how to apply the marketing channels factor to an Internet case. Holding that the factor potentially weighs against the plaintiff because of the unrelatedness of the parties' goods is really conflating this factor with a separate likelihood of confusion factor – competitive proximity of the parties' goods.

Thus, the court's approach to the marketing channels factor leaves something to be desired. It would have been more straightforward for the court to hold, as Judge Nelson did in *Playboy*, that the marketing channels factor should generally carry little weight in Internet cases. In other words, the court in *Bally* could easily have accepted Bally's contention that the marketing channels are the same because both parties utilize the Internet, but then to note that the factor merits little weight because this will be the case in most, if not all, online situations. A revised cyberlaw field would be a useful theoretical arena in which to consider these questions and to come to more comprehensive and reasoned answers than judges can manage on a case-by-case basis.

The Internet has also created other challenges for the application of the likelihood of confusion test. For example, the majority of the court in *Playboy v Netscape* considered the most appropriate ways to arrange the likelihood of confusion analysis in the Internet context. Judge Nelson's opinion raises a number of good points for further consideration of consumer confusion issues when dealing with intermediary liability for online infringement. For one thing, he prioritizes the "evidence of actual confusion" factor even though most circuits numerically consider this factor somewhere in the middle of the list of likelihood of confusion factors. Even though the Ninth Circuit traditionally considers "actual confusion" as the fourth factor, Judge Nelson discusses it first because he feels it is the decisive factor in the case. Based on the survey evidence of actual confusion introduced by the plaintiff, and the fact that actual confusion is at the heart of the likelihood of confusion analysis, Judge

[77] *Id.*, at 1164–65.

Nelson opines that this factor "alone probably suffices to reverse the grant of summary judgment".[78]

Nevertheless, he goes on to consider the other factors in turn: strength of the plaintiff's mark; proximity of the goods; similarity of the marks; marketing channels used (already discussed above); type of goods and degree of consumer care expected; defendant's intent in selecting the mark; likelihood of expansion of the product lines. Several of these fair use factors require a court to compare the plaintiff's goods or services with those of the defendant. This makes sense because the aim of the action is to prevent defendants from marketing goods or services that look like they are sourced by the plaintiff. However, the search engine here is not selling any products or services in competition with the plaintiff. Rather, it is selling keywords to competitors of the plaintiff. Because of this, it might, in fact, have been more sensible for the court to consider this a case of contributory liability on the part of the search engine rather than direct liability.

Because the court considered that direct liability by the search engine was possible, the likelihood of confusion factors requiring a comparison of the parties' respective goods had to be analyzed in a somewhat artificial way – by bringing in the goods of third parties, Playboy's *actual* competitors who bought keywords from Netscape. For example, in considering the "proximity of the goods" factor, Judge Nelson somewhat circuitously states that:

> From an Internet searcher's perspective, the relevant "goods" are the links to the websites being sought and the goods or services available at those sites. The proximity between [Playboy's] and its competitor's goods provides the reason Netscape keys [Playboy's] marks to competitor's banner advertisements in the first place. Accordingly, this factor favors [Playboy] ...[79]

This is a very unusual "proximity of goods" analysis. In a traditional trademark infringement case, a court would compare the plaintiff's and the defendant's goods. However, in this case, the court was forced to do some fast footwork in order to compare the plaintiff's goods with those of third parties who contract with the defendants for sponsored search results. Again, this may suggest that for a more logical analysis the case would have been better decided as one of secondary infringement on the part of the search engine. Of course, this may have increased the cost

[78] *Playboy v Netscape*, *supra* note 1, at 1026.
[79] *Id.*, at 1028.

burden on the plaintiff in having to establish a primary infringement against its direct competitors as a separate part of the action.

The court's result on the "proximity of the goods" factor also negates the need for it to analyze the "likelihood of expansion of product lines" factor, at least according to Judge Nelson: "Because the advertisers' goods and [Playboy's] are already related, as discussed within factor two, this factor is irrelevant".[80] While this analysis of the expansion of product lines issue makes sense in light of the court's analysis of the proximity of goods factor, it does slant the analysis against the search engine. If one bears in mind that the search engine itself is not actually selling any goods in proximity to the plaintiff, but only assisting others in doing so, it is arguably unjust for so many of the "relational" factors in respect of goods to weigh against it. Of course this goes back to the point about whether a search engine should be regarded as directly liable for infringements in these contexts or only potentially secondarily liability.

In the *eBay* litigation discussed above, the court was mindful of not holding certain online intermediaries directly liable for conduct that was instigated by a third party – in that case, the selling of counterfeit goods on eBay's website. The Ninth Circuit took a much dimmer view of Netscape's activities, perhaps because the search engine was actively engaged in selling trademarks for a profit. In that sense *Playboy v Netscape* could perhaps be contrasted with both *eBay* and *1-800-Contacts* on policy grounds related to the extent of the complicity of the online intermediary with the primary infringement. Where an intermediary provides a service that can be used to infringe trademarks, but does its best to monitor and prevent infringements, it arguably should not be liable. This describes the situation in *eBay*. And when an intermediary internally references trademarks but does not sell or communicate them to anyone else, that should equally not amount to infringement, as in the *1-800 Contacts* litigation.

However, when an intermediary's profit model is based on the commercial sale of another's marks, even where that intermediary is not using the mark as an indicator of source for its own products and services, it risks liability. This was the case in *Playboy v Netscape*, although interestingly not so in the *Google France* litigation before the CJEU because the court was unconvinced that the search engine's activities amounted to the kind of "use" that trademark infringement law curtails.

---

80 *Id.*, at 1029.

While in some ways a comparison between these decisions may be inappropriate because they dealt with different aspects of infringement laws amongst different circuits and countries, the analysis does bring several clear issues to light. To date, questions of online trademark infringement have been considered in a piecemeal way by courts in different jurisdictions on a case-by-case basis. This is a perfectly appropriate approach for those courts to take. Their job is to analyze the application of local trademark laws to a given set of facts.

This book advocates a more global theoretical discussion of the attachment of legal liability generally to online intermediaries in areas such as trademark law, copyright law, defamation, privacy and other legal wrongs involving the communication of digital information. The approach advocated here is not intended to displace a consideration of Internet cases within existing fields such as trademark and copyright law, but rather to supplement it.

The advantages of the approach suggested here include the ability to form a more cohesive picture of what is truly going on in cyberspace in terms of legal liabilities attached to online intermediaries, and the various bases upon which liabilities are attached. The discussion highlights inconsistencies in approach between fields of law and between jurisdictions, potentially facilitating the development of more harmonized laws, more well reasoned laws, or simply more awareness between domestic courts and legislatures of all of the issues inherent in attaching liability to online intermediaries. The key issues will largely revolve around balancing innovation by those intermediaries against the need to protect existing legal rights such as trademarks, copyrights, and rights to protect one's privacy and reputation in cyberspace.

3.2.5 Trademark Defenses

In contrast to copyright law, the fair use defense in trademark law at least in the United States is significantly underdeveloped. This might be one area that could be usefully addressed in a cyberlaw field, particularly when considering questions about the extent to which an online intermediary should be held liable for infringements initiated by a third party. As with the balance between the two elements of the infringement action – use in commerce and consumer confusion – a relevant question to ask of trademark defenses is at what point in the litigation they should arise and who should bear the burden of proof.

With respect to the infringement action, the Lanham Act provides that, at least with respect to an incontestable mark, an infringement action is subject to defenses including: "That the use of the name, term, or device charged to be an infringement is a use, *otherwise than as a mark*, of the party's individual name in his own business, or of the individual name of anyone in privity with such party, or of a term or device *which is descriptive of and used fairly and in good faith* only to describe the goods or services of such party, or their geographic origin".[81] (emphasis added) The insertion of the words "otherwise than as a mark" in the fair use defenses to trademark infringement has caused some debate because it is unclear whether these words are intended to qualify the commercial use requirement of the infringement action. If the "commercial use" aspect of infringement means "use as a mark", then arguably this part of the defense is redundant. If the defendant was not using the plaintiff's mark *as a mark* in the first place, there would be no action to which the defense might be applied.

More recently, Congress has amended the statutory defenses relating to trademark dilution and this section is arguably much more clearly articulated than the provision dealing with defenses in the infringement context. With respect to trademark dilution, the Lanham Act provides that:

> The following shall not be actionable as dilution by blurring or dilution by tarnishment under this subsection:
>
> (A) Any *fair use, including a nominative or descriptive fair use*, or facilitation of such fair use, of a famous mark by another person *other than as a designation of source for the person's own goods or services*, including use in connection with –
> (i) advertising or promotion that permits consumers to compare goods or services; or
> (ii) identifying and parodying, criticizing, or commenting upon the famous mark owner or the goods or services of the famous mark owner.
>
> (B) All forms of news reporting and news commentary.
>
> (C) Any noncommercial use of a mark.[82] (emphasis added)

The references to "fair use" in sub-paragraph (A) arguably improve on the fair use defense for infringement in several ways. For one thing, the dilution provision distinguishes between nominative and descriptive fair use. These two classes of fair use have developed at common law, and the relationship between them has occasionally proved confusing in practice. The dilution version of the fair use defense also arguably improves on the

---

81 15 U.S.C. § 1115(b)(4).

82 15 U.S.C. § 1125(c)(3).

infringement version to the extent that it avoids the "otherwise than as a mark" language in the infringement defense. Instead, the dilution provision employs the qualification that the defendant has to have used the mark "other than as a designation of source for the person's own goods or services".

While it is likely that Congress intended to encompass fairly similar concepts in the two provisions, the wording of the dilution provision avoids questions of defining trademark use and focusing instead on whether the defendant is using the mark to designate its own goods in the market place. This may be an easier question for a court to address, particularly in a world where the concept of trademark use is broadening significantly – and arguably encompassing things like merchandising uses as distinct from uses that designate the origin of a specific product or service.

With respect to the distinction between classic fair use and nominative fair use, courts have typically held that the former relates to the use by a defendant of the plaintiff's mark simply in order to describe a quality of the defendant's own goods or services. The obvious examples occur when the plaintiff's mark incorporates a descriptive term (such as "tangy" or "colorful") with secondary meaning,[83] and that descriptive term is necessary for the defendant to use in describing its own product. In the leading Supreme Court case of *K P Permanent*,[84] the term in question was "microcolor" as applied to make-up.[85]

In contrast, nominative fair use is said to occur where the defendant uses the plaintiff's mark to refer to the *plaintiff's* products or services in cases where there is no obvious alternative for the defendant to use.[86] For example, in the *New Kids on the Block* case, the defendant newspaper was running a survey about members of the band New Kids on the Block and there was no other way for it to refer to the band without resorting to use of the plaintiff's own mark.[87] In that case, the Ninth Circuit set out the following test to establish nominative fair use:

> First, the product or service in question must be one not readily identifiable without use of the trademark; second, only so much of the mark or marks may be used as is reasonably necessary to identify the product or service; and

---

83 McCarthy, *supra* note 3, at § 15:5.
84 *K P Permanent v Lasting Impression*, 125 S. Ct. 542 (2004).
85 *Id.*
86 McCarthy, *supra* note 3, at § 31:156.50.
87 *New Kids on the Block v News America*, 971 F.2d 302 (9th Cir. 1992).

> third, the user must do nothing that would, in conjunction with the mark, suggest sponsorship or endorsement by the trademark holder.[88]

Because nominative fair use is in effect a judicial creation, there is a significant variation between courts as to its contours, but this explication suffices for the purposes of the current discussion.[89] While the classic and nominative sub-categories of the trademark fair use defense seem to be quite distinct, there have been cases in which the boundaries between the two are muddied. For example, in *Playboy v Terri Welles*,[90] the defendant was a previous Playmate of the Year in Playboy Magazine. She used Playboy's trademarked terms such as "Playboy" and "Playmate of the Year" to describe herself on her own website. In this sense, she used the terms in a descriptive way to describe *both* her own product and service and the plaintiff's products and services. While the case was ultimately decided under the rubric of nominative fair use, it could easily have been regarded also as a classic fair use case.

In terms of defenses to infringement and dilution actions, questions have also arisen – and have never been uniformly resolved – about the extent to which parody should be regarded as a distinct defense. In the infringement context, some courts have accepted that parody is more properly regarded as relevant to ascertaining consumer confusion on the basis that a parodic use is not a confusing use.[91] However, other courts and commentators have suggested that a specific parody defense is, or should be, accepted in trademark law, potentially on First Amendment grounds.[92]

While a detailed analysis of the ins and out of defenses to trademark infringement and dilution are outside the scope of this discussion, hopefully the above emphasizes the uncertainties inherent in applying the defenses in current trademark law even outside the Internet context. This uncertainty/underdevelopment is both a positive and negative aspect of trademark law from the point of view of examining the contours of trademarks in cyberspace. While uncertainty can lead to inconsistency, it can also provide the flexibility for scholars and judges engaged in cyberlaw questions to formulate approaches that make sense in online

---

88 *Id.*, at 308.

89 The test for nominative fair use was further refined in later cases. See, for example, *Century 21 Real Estate Corp. v Lendingtree, Inc.*, 425 F.3d 211, 76 U.S.P.Q.2d 1769 (3d Cir. 2005); MCCARTHY, *supra* note 3, at § 31:156.50.

90 279 F.3d 796 (9th Cir. 2002).

91 MCCARTHY, *supra* note 3, at § 31:153.

92 *Id.*

cases. To what extent should intermediaries such as search engines and online retailers be put to the proof of a trademark defense? What are reasonable burdens to impose on such intermediaries in trademark cases? This is fruitful ground for cyberlawyers to explore.

We saw in the previous chapter that, in the copyright context, the burdens imposed on online intermediaries in raising fair use defenses are becoming established, taking into account the need to promote innovation in online services. For example, the concept of transformative use under the first factor of the statutory fair use test now clearly encompasses functional uses such as presenting thumbnail images in search results. It would now be beneficial if similar developments took place with respect to trademark law.

3.2.6 Trademark Dilution

Trademark dilution is a separate action, distinct from infringement. It does not require a showing of consumer confusion, although it does retain the commercial use requirement mirroring that in the infringement action. Dilution comes in two forms: blurring and tarnishment. Both forms are expressly recognized at the federal level in the Lanham Act.[93] Dilution by blurring is defined as: "association arising from the similarity between a mark or trade name and a famous mark that impairs the distinctiveness of the famous mark".[94] Dilution by tarnishment is defined as: "association arising from the similarity between a mark or trade name and a famous mark that harms the reputation of the famous mark".[95] Both provisions require the plaintiff to establish the existence of a "famous mark" which is defined in the Lanham Act as follows:

> [a] mark is famous if it is widely recognized by the general consuming public of the United States as a designation of source of the goods or services of the mark's owner. In determining whether a mark possesses the requisite degree of recognition, the court may consider all relevant factors, including the following:
>
> (i) The duration, extent, and geographic reach of advertising and publicity of the mark, whether advertised or publicized by the owner or third parties.
> (ii) The amount, volume, and geographic extent of sales of goods or services offered under the mark.
> (iii) The extent of actual recognition of the mark … .

---

93 17 U.S.C. § 1125(c).
94 17 U.S.C. § 1125(c)(2)(B).
95 17 U.S.C. § 1125(c)(2)(C).

The legislative intent is to protect those who have spent sufficient resources building up a substantial brand from uses of the same or similar marks on different products in circumstances that might harm the distinguishing power of the brand (blurring) or the reputation of the mark (tarnishment). An example of blurring would be to use a famous mark like Kodak on a product not associated with photography: say, Kodak pianos. While consumers may not be confused by such a use for infringement purposes, it may nevertheless cause "noise" around the brand that interferes with the mark's distinctiveness. An example of tarnishment would be to use the mark on, say, sexually explicit material like Kodak x-rated videos.

Dilution can be argued alongside infringement on the same facts, if the facts support both actions, or it can be a stand-alone action. The typical dilution cases that have arisen in cyberspace have involved Internet domain names. Sometimes these are cases where the plaintiff raises more than one trademark-related cause of action, and sometimes they are pure dilution cases. Dilution was particularly attractive to plaintiffs in the early days of online commerce when the first instances of cybersquatting came to light: that is, cases where a defendant registered a domain name corresponding with a plaintiff's mark in order to extort money from the plaintiff for transfer of the domain name. While cybersquatting issues are now typically handled more cheaply and efficiently under the UDRP, in the early days of the Internet, prior to the implementation of the UDRP, dilution actions proved useful to plaintiffs seeking to protect their valuable marks in the domain space.

Consider, for example, the oft-cited case of *Panavision v Toeppen*.[96] The defendant – Dennis Toeppen – was a high-profile early cybersquatter who registered domain names comprising multiple trademarks in the hope of selling them to trademark holders for a profit. When Panavision sued him over his registration of the "Panavision.com" name, they framed the case as a dilution action because there was nothing Toeppen was doing that could be said to be confusing consumers for the purposes of trademark infringement. An Internet user accessing the "Panavision-.com" domain was confronted by photographs of the town of Pana, Illinois rather than anything that could be associated with the trademark holder. In order to establish dilution (by blurring in this case), Panavision had to establish that Toeppen's use of Panavision's mark was a commercial use and that it satisfied that statutory test for blurring – a prior

---

[96] 141 F.3d 1316 (9th Cir. 1998).

version of the current statute. However, differences between the two versions of the statute are not particularly relevant to this discussion.

The Ninth Circuit held in favor of Panavision. The court regarded Toeppen's activities as comprising a commercial use under the dilution statute because registering domain names for profit was Toeppen's business and thus he was engaged in a commercial activity involving his attempts to sell the domains to corresponding trademark holders.[97] Additionally, his activities were preventing the rightful trademark holders from commercially exploiting their valuable marks in corresponding domain names.[98]

In considering whether Toeppen's use of Panavision's mark actually diluted Panavision's capacity to use its marks to identify its own goods and services, the court engaged in a discussion of the significance of Internet domain names to electronic commerce. At the time the case was decided, search engines were nowhere near as sophisticated as they are today and Internet users relied heavily on guessing intuitive domain names and typing them directly into their Internet browsers. The court relied heavily on Toeppen's apparent incursion into Panavision's legitimate online address space to support a claim of dilution by blurring.

While this case does not discuss the potential liability of any online intermediaries, it does exemplify what courts have typically done when confronted with Internet issues for the first time in a given context. In seeking to balance existing trademark rights against innovative uses of technology (the new domain name system), the court was easily able to make the line call in favor of protecting the trademark rights. There was no overall policy or practical gain from protecting otherwise wasteful/ extortive uses of domain names over and above protecting markholder's rights. Allowing markholders the ability to secure their marks in domain spaces would facilitate the development of electronic commerce and efficient use of Internet domain names in that context. Protecting cybersquatters would likely chill both of those ends.

Most of the case law on dilution involving Internet domain names involves the primary liability of a domain name registrant, rather than the intermediary liability of a search engine or domain name registrar. There are a number of reasons why the defendants in these cases have tended to be the direct participants in the dilution, rather than the online intermediaries whose services are used to facilitate the dilution. Some of these

---

97 *Id.*, at 1325.

98 *Id.*

reasons are discussed in the final section of this chapter which specifically focuses on Internet domain name issues.

Courts have occasionally been prepared to impose liability on domain name registrars for the tortious activities of registrants, but these have been unique and unusual cases, and have generally not been cases involving trademarks. For example, in the case of *Kremen v Cohen*,[99] the Ninth Circuit was prepared to attach liability to Network Solutions for agreeing to transfer the incredibly valuable "sex.com" domain name to a con man who forged a letter allegedly from the original registrant agreeing to the transfer. This scenario differed from a trademark case in that liability was not being attached to the registrar for failure to be aware of a plaintiff's trademark rights, but rather for accepting a forged transfer letter without contacting the putative transferor to doublecheck the veracity of the letter. It would have been a very simple matter for the registrar to undertake such a check – a single email would have sufficed. So the court was prepared to attach liability on this basis under Californian conversion law.[100]

Domain name disputes are especially interesting for a conception of cyberlaw because of the ways in which intermediary liability has generally been avoided through contractual dispute resolution procedures. These methods are examined in the next section. The point of this section has been to introduce the key aspects of trademark law that have arisen in the Internet context and the ways in which courts have faced the balance between the protection of existing intellectual property rights against the need to encourage online innovation. To the extent that these situations have involved online intermediaries and their business models, the main focus has been on the key aspects of the trademark infringement action – commercial use and consumer confusion. These are areas which, along with trademark defenses, should be examined and developed in a reconceptualized cyberlaw field focused on promoting the innovative practices of online intermediaries, while retaining the ability to protect intellectual property rights online.

---

99 337 F.3d 1024 (2002).

100 *Id.*, at 1035–36 ("Given that Network Solutions's 'regulations' evidently allowed it to hand over a registrant's domain name on the basis of a facially suspect letter without even contacting him, 'further regulations' don't seem like such a bad idea. And the prospect of higher fees presents no issue here that it doesn't in any other context. A bank could lower its ATM fees if it didn't have to pay security guards, but we doubt most depositors would think that was a good idea").

3.3 TRADEMARKS, DOMAIN NAMES, AND INNOVATIVE APPROACHES TO CYBERSPACE REGULATION

3.3.1 Challenges Inherent in Domain Name Litigation

3.3.1.1 Jurisdictional challenges

The advent of the Internet domain name system brought new pressures to bear on trademark law, both in terms of the letter of the law itself and in terms of the results of conflicts involving domain name registrations. Domain name disputes, particularly those involving trademarks, raised important new challenges. Because of the global nature of the Internet addressing system, jurisdiction was a potential problem since its inception. Plaintiffs and defendants are often located in different jurisdictions, and cross-border litigation is difficult and costly.

Substantive laws can also differ between jurisdictions. While trademark laws are relatively well harmonized across national borders, there are some distinct differences which could lead to vastly different results depending on which jurisdiction's laws are applied to a dispute. For example, if a defendant cybersquatter registers a trademark corresponding to the plaintiff's mark in a filing-based trademark jurisdiction, she would arguably be in a position to claim a trademark right that would not necessarily be available in a use-based system such as the United States. Some countries' trademark laws allow those who register a mark to claim a property or property-like interest in the mark from the date of registration while others condition the rights on use of the mark in commerce.

One solution to the jurisdictional challenges raised by early domain name disputes was enacting legislation to allow *in rem* jurisdiction based on the domain name as a property right in and of itself. That at least avoids problems inherent in applying principles of personal jurisdiction to a foreign defendant. The United States Congress took this approach to *in rem* jurisdiction over domain name disputes involving trademarks under the ACPA. This legislation inserted *in rem* provisions into the cybersquatting provisions of the Lanham Act that would apply in circumstances where it was difficult or impossible for a plaintiff trademark holder to assert *in personam* jurisdiction over a foreign defendant.[101] Most jurisdictions did not go to this effort in dealing with domain name disputes, leaving it to courts to decide when, and on what basis,

---

[101] 15 U.S.C. § 1125(d)(2).

jurisdiction over a domain name dispute should be exercised. Even in the United States, the *in rem* provisions of the ACPA have not been often argued in practice.

3.3.1.2 Substantive challenges relating to the role of domain name registrars

Outside of the jurisdictional challenges raised for courts in early domain name litigation were challenges inherent in characterizing the role of the domain name registrar in circumstances where the registrant either could not be found or could not be brought within the court's jurisdiction. As with any other online intermediary, an action brought against a domain name registrar is often cheaper, faster and more likely to be effective than an action brought against a direct infringer. The location of the registrar is easily ascertained and, in the early days of the Internet, all the most valuable domain names – those in the ".com", ".net" and ".org" spaces – were registered by Network Solutions in Herndon, Virginia. An action successfully brought against a registrar would have the immediate effect of cancellation or transfer of the disputed domain name and this remedy could be quickly and easily implemented by the registrar as the body with control over registration of the relevant name.

The decision of who to sue in the early days of domain name disputes was not necessarily a difficult one, and the benefits of litigating against a registrar were obvious. What was less obvious was the best way to argue the claim. While a registrar may assist a primary infringer by allowing it to register a domain name corresponding with another's mark, the registrar itself has not likely infringed or diluted the mark. An argument might be made that a registrar's acceptance of an application for registration by, say, a cybersquatter is a commercial use of the mark in the trademark sense, particularly if "commercial use" does not narrowly connote a "trademark use". However, nothing the registrar itself does is likely to create a substantial likelihood of consumer confusion for infringement purposes, nor is its conduct likely to cause blurring or tarnishment for dilution purposes. It may *facilitate* another party engaging in these activities, but all the registrar does is accept payment and license the name to the applicant for registration. For example, in one of the more notable examples of early domestic litigation against Network Solutions for trademark infringement, *Lockheed Martin v Network Solutions*, the District Court for the Central District of California held that Network Solutions was not directly liable for infringement or dilution because the Internet addressing services it provided to third party infringers were not "commercial uses" as contemplated in the Lanham Act.[102]

The Ninth Circuit Court of Appeals later considered the extent to which Network Solutions might be held liable for contributory infringement with respect to third party infringements caused by registration of domain names relating to the plaintiff's "Skunk Works" trademarks.[103] The court held against contributory infringement, relying heavily on the *Inwood* conception of contributory infringement.[104] As readers will recall from the above discussion, the *Inwood* formulation states that: "Contributory infringement occurs when the defendant either intentionally induces a third party to infringe the plaintiff's mark or supplies a product to a third party with actual or constructive knowledge that the product is being used to infringe the service mark".[105]

The Ninth Circuit noted that Lockheed Martin agreed that there was no intentional inducement of infringement when the registrar merely provides an addressing service to third parties who may or may not infringe others' trademarks. Thus, the case was argued solely on the basis of supplying a product or service to a third party with actual or constructive knowledge that the product or service is being used to infringe a mark.[106] The court quickly characterized Network Solutions' activities as providing a service, rather than a product. The development of an Internet addressing system under which Network Solutions accepts applications to map an applicant's Internet Protocol address to a particular mnemonic term is not, according to the court, a physical product, but rather an addressing service not unlike the addressing service provided by the United States Postal Service.[107]

---

[102] *Lockheed Martin v Network Solutions*, 985 F. Supp. 949 (1997).

[103] *Lockheed Martin v Network Solutions*, 194 F.3d 980 (1999).

[104] *Id.*, at 983–84.

[105] *Id.*, at 983.

[106] *Id.* ("Lockheed alleges only the latter basis for contributory infringement liability and therefore must prove that NSI supplies a product to third parties with actual or constructive knowledge that its product is being used to infringe 'Skunk Works'").

[107] *Id.*, at 984–85 ("The case at bench involves a fact pattern squarely on the 'service' side of the product/service distinction suggested by *Inwood Lab* and its offspring. All evidence in the record indicates that NSI's role differs little from that of the United States Postal Service: when an Internet user enters a domain-name combination, NSI translates the domain-name combination to the registrant's IP Address and routes the information or command to the corresponding computer. Although NSI's routing service is only available to a

This analogy is a little inaccurate in the sense that the USPS does not "create" the street address to begin with, but merely routes mail there, while Network Solutions arguably does create the ability of the primary infringer to use the mnemonic address. Whether or not this characterization of Network Solutions' services is accurate, the court further held that Network Solutions was not in a position to directly control and monitor the primary infringer's activities.[108] This observation is probably the crux of the case. While the court did not make the point expressly, it would be unwieldy to expect Internet domain name registrars to conduct monitoring and control over every domain name registrant to ensure that they are not infringing another's marks. Network Solutions, and later other registrars, would neither have the expertise nor the resources to undertake such a task, at least not while maintaining a cost-effective domain name system.

It could be argued that the monitoring and control burden should not be applied to monitoring and controlling what a registrant actually *does* with a domain name post-registration, but rather to the application to register the name itself. In other words, one could impose a burden on domain name registrars to ensure that applicants for registration are not planning to infringe another's mark or are not seeking to register a domain name corresponding to another's mark at all. However, this task would also be unwieldy and economically ineffective if not impossible while maintaining an accessible, low-cost domain name system. Asking registrars to ascertain whether an applicant was planning to infringe another's trademark rights would be an impossible burden for them to bear. This would be a particularly tall order, bearing in mind the global nature of the domain name system and the multiple variations of registered and unregistered marks in every country.

Ultimately, a more elegant solution to the challenge of protecting trademarks in the domain space was developed by ICANN under the auspices of the UDRP. If this had not occurred, it is possible that courts would have started to take a more aggressive stance against trademark infringement and dilution, possibly extending liability to domain name

---

registrant who has paid NSI's fee, NSI does not supply the domain-name combination any more than the Postal Service supplies a street address by performing the routine service of routing mail").

[108] *Id.*, at 985 ("The 'direct control and monitoring' rule established by *Hard Rock* and *Fonovisa* likewise fails to reach the instant situation. The district court correctly recognized that NSI's rote translation service does not entail the kind of direct control and monitoring required to justify an extension of the 'supplies a product' requirement").

registrars. For example, offering to sell domain name registrations for a profit might be likened to keyword advertising which has been regarded as a commercial use for infringement purposes under the Lanham Act.[109] Even if this occurred, a plaintiff would still have to prove the other elements of either infringement or dilution. Nevertheless, that may not be an impossible task.

However, the UDRP has taken the pressure off domestic courts to develop trademark law precedents involving Internet domain names. It has also demonstrated that private solutions to cyberspace challenges, especially those involving online intermediaries, are possible at least in some circumstances. Thus, a study of the UDRP – along with other initiatives developed more recently by ICANN[110] – is an important aspect of cyberlaw.

3.3.2 The UDRP as an Alternative Approach to Online Dispute Resolution

The UDRP is an impressive achievement in online dispute resolution, and it may serve as a model for future approaches to dispute resolution. However, one of the things that makes it possible is the structure of the Internet domain name system relying, as it does, on a network of domain name registries who are in a position to impose contractual terms on registrants. As with all other areas of law, the most effective way to create an alternative dispute resolution mechanism to which parties are required to adhere is through contract. It is only because the entire domain name system is premised on a series of contracts – contracts between ICANN and registrars authorizing them to administer registries, and contracts between registrars and registrants – that such an effective global system of private dispute resolution is possible.

The UDRP was implemented in 1999 as a fast, efficient, low-cost, online avenue for resolving domain name disputes involving unauthorized registration and use of domain names corresponding to complainants' marks. It applies to both registered and unregistered marks, and is incorporated into all registration agreements for ".com", ".net", ".org" and a number of other domain spaces. The system enables trademark holders to have low-cost effective recourse to protection of their marks in the domain space without having to resort to domestic litigation and all of its associated cost and jurisdictional challenges.

---

[109] *Playboy v Netscape*, 354 F.3d 1020 (2004); *Rescuecom v Google*, 562 F.3d 123 (2009).

[110] See note 23, *supra*.

What is less often mentioned in the literature is that the UDRP nicely addresses the problem of intermediary liability by contractually imposing the burden on the applicant for registration of a domain name to represent and warrant that she is not infringing on anyone else's rights. This is made abundantly clear in Clause 2 of the UDRP:

> By applying to register a domain name, or by asking us to maintain or renew a domain name registration, you hereby represent and warrant to us that: (a) the statements that you made in your Registration Agreement are complete and accurate; (b) to your knowledge, the registration of the domain name will not infringe upon or otherwise violate the rights of any third party; (c) you are not registering the domain name for an unlawful purpose; and (d) you will not knowingly use the domain name in violation of any applicable laws or regulations. It is your responsibility to determine whether your domain name registration infringes or violates someone else's rights.

The UDRP then goes on to require the registrant – the "you" in the agreement – to submit to a mandatory administrative proceeding if a third party complainant lodges a UDRP complaint about the registration of the domain name:

> You are required to submit to a mandatory administrative proceeding in the event that a third party (a "complainant") asserts … that
>
> (i) your domain name is identical or confusingly similar to a trademark or service mark in which the complainant has rights; and
> (ii) you have no rights or legitimate interests in respect of the domain name; and
> (iii) your domain name has been registered and is being used in bad faith.[111]

The policy goes on to define the terms introduced in these provisions including the concept of "bad faith" and the kinds of issues a registrant can raise to defend against the complaint and establish a legitimate use of the name. While the UDRP also acknowledges, as indeed it must, that a contractual arrangement such as this cannot oust the jurisdiction of the courts,[112] it has been a wildly successful avenue for domain name dispute resolution in practice. Most domain name disputes are handled through

---

[111] Uniform Domain Name Dispute Resolution Policy, cl. 4(a).

[112] *Id.*, at cl. 4(k) ("The mandatory administrative proceeding requirements set forth in Paragraph 4 shall not prevent either you or the complainant from submitting the dispute to a court of competent jurisdiction for independent resolution before such mandatory administrative proceeding is commenced or after such proceeding is concluded").

the UDRP rather than in domestic courts, and the numbers of UDRP disputes rise exponentially every year.[113]

As trademark holders can now generally obtain relief under the UDRP, they will typically not resort to domestic litigation, which in turn reduces the likelihood that any actions will be brought against domain name registrars. Even if a trademark holder was minded to bring action against a registrar, the provisions of Clause 2 of the UDRP would give the registrar some comfort, if not deter the complainant altogether. Where the registrar takes the trouble of obtaining warranties from applicants that they are not infringing another's legal rights, it is difficult for a potential plaintiff to argue that the registrar is not sufficiently monitoring the activities of its registrants with an eye to trademark litigation.

The success of the UDRP both in terms of streamlining disputes between trademark holders and primary infringers, and in terms of minimizing potential registrar liability for trademark actions, is a great achievement for ICANN. It demonstrates that there may be alternative methods to ensure low-cost innovation in cyberspace while at the same time protecting legal interests such as trademark rights. The UDRP protects innovation in domain name registration by keeping costs and legal liabilities under control for those providing registration and associated services, while at the same time providing a cost-effective trademark-protection avenue for markholders.

The challenge for the cyberlaw of the future is that this kind of success and balance is difficult to replicate outside the domain space because of the specific elements of the domain name system that lend themselves to contractually-based alternative dispute resolution mechanisms. While some online intermediaries can utilize contracts to minimize their potential legal liability, many cannot. For example, online social media services generally require members to sign contracts when establishing an account, and those contracts will require the new member to agree to terms of service that include agreements not to infringe others' legal rights.[114] These terms of service typically incorporate intellectual property rights – notably copyright and trademark rights – as well as some privacy and defamation concerns.[115]

---

[113] See http://www.wipo.int/amc/en/domains/statistics/, last viewed on June 30, 2014.

[114] See, for example, Facebook's Terms of Service, cl. 6 (available at: https://www.facebook.com/legal/terms, last viewed on June 30, 2014).

[115] See, for example, The Twitter Rules, available at https://support.twitter.com/articles/18311-the-twitter-rules#, last viewed on June 30, 2014.

However, many online intermediaries do not utilize contracts for everyday users. Internet search engines, for example, will require contracts for keyword advertisers, but not for individuals who simply use their services for online searches. Many blogs do not require commenters to sign membership forms in order to participate in discussions. Developing contractual solutions to minimize intermediary liability will be a key part of the cyberlaw of the future. Arguably insufficient attention has been paid to this issue in the cyberlaw field to date. However, in many circumstances, notably those in which the defendant has no contractual relationship with the online intermediary, or where the contract doesn't reach the activity of which a plaintiff complains, separate legal regulation may be required. Additionally, the UDRP effectively contains built-in and immediately effective enforcement mechanisms, an aspect of the system that may not be easily replicable in other cyberspace contexts. In the UDRP context, this effective enforcement arises because the very registrars that maintain registrations have the power – and are required and willing – to cancel or transfer a domain name registration when ordered to do so by a UDRP arbitrator or panel of arbitrators.

4. Online defamation and other harmful speech

4.1 DEFAMATION IN CYBERSPACE

4.1.1 Digital Challenges for Defamation Law

4.1.1.1 Jurisdiction

As with the digital challenges posed to intellectual property law, defamation law soon felt pressure from the emerging global communications medium in the last decade of the 20th century. Defamation was an obvious pressure point for Internet regulation because defamation is an information-based tort, and information can cross global boundaries almost instantaneously at the push of a button. Unlike intellectual property law, defamation is not based on the protection of property rights in information. Rather, it is concerned with the protection of individuals' reputations that may be harmed by communications published by one or more defendants. The concern here is not with appropriating information as property, but in harming reputations. Nevertheless, the common threads for the purposes of cyberlaw are that defamation deals with purely information-based torts, and online the communication of information requires intermediaries.

Because of the nature of the Internet as a global intermediated communications network, defamation law in the early 1990s was immediately faced with jurisdictional issues as well as concerns about the extent to which various entities in the chain of publication of defamatory content should be held responsible for the harms caused. While this book does not focus on jurisdictional issues as a mainstay of cyberlaw, given that jurisdictional issues have been relatively easily resolved in practice within domestic courts, defamation law is a good example of how courts have dealt with these issues. Concerns about imposing personal jurisdiction over a foreign defendant have in many ways been secondary to concerns about the appropriate law to apply to a given defendant. Entities that publish information globally on the Internet can reasonably be brought to account in any place in which their publication causes damage. Courts in countries that take a strict due process view on when it would be fair to hale a defendant into a foreign court tend to agree that one who has published harmful material knowing the harm would be felt in another jurisdiction can rightfully be expected to defend their actions in that place.[1]

Where the jurisdictional problems for defamation law are perhaps more pronounced are in cases where the substantive defamation rules vary widely between different countries. In other words, the outcome of a choice of law challenge can be determinative of major variations in a plaintiff's likelihood of success. For example, while it is very difficult – if not impossible in many cases – for public figures to bring defamation suits in the United States, such individuals routinely bring such actions, and succeed, in Australia.[2] These differences largely stem from constitutional differences underpinning the defamation laws in each jurisdiction. While the United States has a highly developed First Amendment jurisprudence which effectively limits a public figure's right to quell critical speech, Australia has no express constitutional guarantee of free speech. There is no constitutional impediment to public figures bringing defamation actions, except in very narrow circumstances.[3]

The substance of other information-based tort laws might also vary significantly between jurisdictions such that a jurisdictional challenge could potentially prevent a plaintiff from achieving redress on substantive law grounds. In other words, a plaintiff who cannot establish jurisdiction

---

[1] See, for example, *Gutnick v Dow Jones*, [2002] HCA 56; para. 186 ("If people wish to do business in, or indeed travel to, or live in, or utilise the infrastructure of different countries, they can hardly expect to be absolved from compliance with the laws of those countries. The fact that publication might occur everywhere does not mean that it occurs nowhere. Multiple publication in different jurisdictions is certainly no novelty in a federation such as Australia").

[2] See discussion in *The News Manual: Defamation in Australia*, available at http://www.thenewsmanual.net/Resources/medialaw_in_australia_02.html, last viewed on June 30, 2014, noting the limited reach of the public figure defense in Australia as compared to the United States ("Two rulings by the High Court introduced a new defence based on what the judges saw as an implied freedom of speech in the Constitution. The High Court decided (by a majority decision) that in order for democracy to work, we must be allowed to say defamatory things about people engaged in political debate without fear of being sued if they prove to be untrue. The defence is similar to the so-called 'public figure defence' available in the United States, but only applies in cases of genuine political discussions (which the High Court left lower courts to define) and it cannot be used to defame people simply because they are in the public eye").

[3] *Id.*

in one country may be unable to bring a substantive action in another if the substantive law of that other country does not provide the same legal rights as her home country. This occurred with respect to the "misappropriation" limb of privacy law in the case of *Chang v Virgin Mobile*.[4] The plaintiff – an American situated in Texas – sought to bring a privacy tort claim against an Australian company who had used her likeness without authorization in a series of advertisements published in Australia. The United States District Court for the Northern District of Texas held that the proper forum for the dispute was Australia. This holding effectively deprived the plaintiff of a remedy as the misappropriation privacy tort is not available under Australian tort law. Even if the plaintiff had the wherewithal to litigate in Australia, there would have been no substantive cause of action that would be equivalent to the claim she could have made in Texas.

While this chapter focuses specifically on defamation, and following chapters delve more deeply into privacy and other information-based torts, it is worth noting at the outset that information-based torts tend to vary more widely in their scope from jurisdiction to jurisdiction than information property (or intellectual property) torts. Intellectual property legislation tends to be enacted largely at the federal level, as opposed to defamation, privacy, and cyber-harassment laws. Additionally, intellectual property laws are relatively well harmonized by international treaties such as TRIPs,[5] the Berne Convention,[6] and the Paris Convention.[7] Defamation, privacy and other information-based torts tends to be more fragmented in substance between countries, and even between states and provinces within federal jurisdictions. Thus, the determination of a jurisdictional challenge, either on the appropriate choice of forum or the appropriate choice of law, potentially has a greater impact on the plaintiff than would be the case in, say, a copyright or trademark case.

4.1.1.2 Online intermediaries

Another obvious challenge for defamation law in the digital age has been the determination of who ultimately bears responsibility for publication of defamatory content. In a system in which so many intermediaries may be involved in the chain of publication, many of whom would not necessarily be aware of the content in question, the extent to which

---

4 U.S. Dist. LEXIS 3051 (2009).

5 Agreement on Trade-Related Aspects of Intellectual Property Rights (TRIPS) (1994).

6 Berne Convention for the Protection of Literary and Artistic Works (1886).

7 Paris Convention for the Protection of Industrial Property (1883).

liability might, or should, attach to those intermediaries becomes problematic. Copyright law has faced similar challenges in the digital age. As the network is made up of conduits that retransmit, cache, and serve as forums for posting information, the extent to which liability attaches to those entities has profound ramifications for the cost of innovation within the system. If those with no intent to harm or little ability to know about or manage harm are saddled with legal liability, their innovative technological activities may be challenged. However, if those entities can innovate free of any risk of legal responsibility, many may be deprived of existing legal rights, not the least of which are rights to protect one's valuable copyrights and one's reputation in the digital age.

As we saw in Chapter 2, copyright law has struggled to maintain an equilibrium between facilitating online innovation and protecting existing intellectual property rights. As new technologies are developed, the balance needs to be continually revisited, particularly in terms of doctrines involving secondary liability and available defenses. The United States Congress has implemented some protection for online service providers against copyright liability under the guise of the OCILLA.[8]

The need to balance defamation law against online innovation has led to some similar legislative initiatives in the United States, notably under § 230 of the Communications Decency Act (CDA) which is discussed below. Interestingly, the balance with respect to Internet service provider liability for defamatory – and other harmful – content posted online has been struck in a different policy place to that involving copyright liability. The reasons for this are discussed below.

4.2 INTERMEDIARY LIABILITY FOR DEFAMATION LAW

4.2.1 The Paradox of Intermediary Liability

As with other areas of law in the digital age, although there are plenty of examples of plaintiffs bringing defamation actions against primary infringers, there are also many cases where the plaintiff seeks an alternative defendant because the primary infringer – the person who originally authored the content – is in another jurisdiction, is difficult to identify or locate, or is impecunious. The author of the defamatory content may also not be the person in the most effective position to curtail the spread of

[8] See discussion in Part 2.3.3, *supra*.

the defamatory content if the court orders an injunction. An online service provider, on the other hand, may be a more attractive defendant for several reasons. An injunction against an online publisher of defamatory content may effectively shut down a major source of the information – although on the Internet, content spreads like wildfire at the best of times. Additionally, online service providers may be easier to locate and to serve, and may have the financial wherewithal to satisfy a damages award.

The problem is that online intermediaries are not necessarily the kinds of publishers that have typically been held liable for defamation in the physical world. Defamation liability in the physical world has typically been limited to those who author the content as well as those who publish it such as traditional media outlets – radio broadcasters, television newscasters, newspapers. While these traditional media companies now operate online and are often the subject of defamation proceedings, they have been joined by many other categories of online publishers who may not appropriately be held to the same standards as journalists and traditional publishers.

Defamatory content may appear on online bulletin boards, in online chatrooms, and via online social networks such as Facebook. While many of these entities technically publish information, they are typically not involved in the journalistic enterprise to the same extent as traditional media outlets. At this point it is worth noting that, unlike the previous discussion of copyright and trademark law, we are not here talking about primary versus secondary liability considerations for online publishers. Rather, we are talking about the concept of "publishing" that attaches primary liability to the activities of anyone who publishes defamatory content. The questions that have arisen in the defamation context relating to online service providers are thus predominantly primary liability questions – the extent to which the service provider can be considered a "publisher" under traditional defamation law.

The decision to hold an online service provider who is not a traditional media outlet liable can have significant repercussions for the flow of online speech and the availability of innovative online communications services. Limiting liability to traditional media outlets maintains the advantages inherent in a system where those defendants generally have lawyers on staff and are generally familiar with journalistic codes of ethics. Thus, the defamation playing field is more level when cases are litigated between these defendants and aggrieved plaintiffs. When the potential playing field expands to include defendants with lesser knowledge of defamation law and journalistic ethics, the burdens of imposing liability on new kinds of intermediaries could result in those entities shutting down innovative services or refraining from releasing those services in the first place. However, that is not to say that individual reputations should not go unprotected online. It is unfair to say that anything goes on the Internet simply because this is a new form of communications medium.

One of the early problems in defamation law online – becoming apparent in American courts in the early 1990s – was that the existing defamation laws did not provide logical incentives for online service providers to monitor content and protect individuals from harmful communications. In cyberlaw courses, professors often teach the *Cubby v CompuServe*[9] and *Stratton Oakmont v Prodigy*[10] cases side-by-side to illustrate this point. These cases represent the state of American defamation law prior to the enactment of § 230 of the CDA. It is necessary to consider the pre-§ 230 law in order to properly understand what Congress was attempting to achieve with the law.

In *Cubby*, the District Court for the Southern District of New York was faced with an early defamation case involving the posting of defamatory content on bulletin boards that were hosted by CompuServe. As a major Internet service provider, CompuServe hosted a lot of such bulletin boards where people freely posted content, some of it defamatory, without CompuServe having specific knowledge of all content posted. Due to the volume of messages posted on its services, it would have been very difficult – if not impossible – for CompuServe to monitor all postings on all the bulletin boards it hosted.

Ultimately holding that CompuServe was not liable for the defamatory content, the court grappled with distinctions in domestic defamation law between "publisher" and "distributor" liability for defamatory content. Historically, distributors – such as libraries and newsstands – have been held to a lower standard of liability than those who actually publish defamatory content such as media companies. The allegories between the digital world and the physical world in this case serve as a stark reminder that even in the tangible world, there is a chain of publication in which some entities that do not actually put pen to paper, or broadcaster to microphone, nevertheless engage in the spread of damaging content. Defamation law has historically dealt with those who play a lesser role in the chain – in other words, those not actually involved in the publication of harmful material, but only its subsequent distribution – by imposing lesser standards of liability.

---

9 776 F. Supp. 135 (S.D.N.Y. 1991).

10 1995 WL 323710 (N.Y. Sup. Ct. May 24, 1995).

As the CompuServe court acknowledged, defamation law requires that "a distributor must have knowledge of the contents of a publication before liability can be imposed for distributing that publication".[11] Distributors include entities like libraries, newsstands, bookstores and the like: those that distribute large volumes of content without necessarily being aware of the details of every book or journal passing through their hands. The question for the court in *Cubby* was whether the online service provider was more appropriately regarded as a publisher or a distributor of the content on the bulletin boards. In some ways it resembled a traditional publisher in that the harmful content was actually published on a web service that it operated. However, in other ways, it resembled a distributor in that it had little say or control over the nature of the content.

In holding that the latter characterization best described CompuServe's activities, the court noted that: "While CompuServe may decline to carry a given publication altogether, in reality, once it does decide to carry a publication, it will have little or no editorial control over that publication's contents. This is especially so when CompuServe carries the publication as part of a forum that is managed by a company unrelated to CompuServe".[12]

In making its holding, the court likened the services provided by CompuServe to those provided by a public library, bookstore or newsstand in that "it would be no more feasible for CompuServe to examine every publication it carries for potentially defamatory statements than it would be for any other distributor to do so".[13] The court appeared mindful of the need to balance online innovation against legal liability for defamation. In several places in the judgment the court recognizes the importance of technological innovation such as that provided by CompuServe, commenting that "CompuServe and companies like it are at the forefront of the information industry revolution".[14] Ultimately, in terms of the appropriate standard of liability to be applied to an online intermediary such as CompuServe, the court expressly stated that:

> Technology is rapidly transforming the information industry. A computerized database is the functional equivalent of a more traditional news vendor, and the inconsistent application of a lower standard of liability to an electronic news distributor such as CompuServe than that which is applied to a public

---

11 *Cubby v Compuserve*, 776 F. Supp. 135, 139 (1991).

12 *Id.*, at 140.

13 *Id.*

14 *Id.*

library, book store, or newsstand would impose an undue burden on the free flow of information.[15]

Ultimately the court held that the appropriate standard for liability for an intermediary such as CompuServe is whether it "knew or had reason to know of the allegedly defamatory" content.[16] On the facts presented to the court it was not clear that CompuServe did have sufficient knowledge of the defamatory content, resulting in a grant of summary judgment in favor of CompuServe.

While this decision seems simple enough to understand, a paradox was created by the subsequent decision in *Prodigy*. In this case, the operator of a computer network that advertised itself as being family friendly came under judicial consideration. When defamatory comments were posted on its services, it sought to avail itself of the holding in *Cubby*, but the court distinguished the case on its facts, and held Prodigy liable for the defamatory comments initiated by others on its bulletin boards.

The basis for the distinction between the two factual scenarios was that, not only did Prodigy hold itself out as being family friendly, but it had a number of procedures in place to ensure that content posted on its services was safe and appropriate. These procedures included the imposition of content guidelines that requested users of the services to refrain from posting damaging material, software screening programs that pre-screened user postings for offensive language, and board leaders who were trained to manage online content and could use emergency delete functions to remove such content.[17] Prodigy argued that many of these procedures had turned out to be not cost-effective and it had ceased utilizing them before the content in question was posted. However, it was not clear that Prodigy had communicated this fact to the public, or its users, effectively at any point. Thus, Prodigy was effectively reaping the financial benefits associated with advertising itself as a family friendly Internet service provider while at the same time failing to provide that service.

The court applied the *Cubby* precedent to Prodigy's activities and held that Prodigy should be classed as a "publisher" rather than as a "distributor" of content. While a distributor is "a passive conduit"[18] of harmful material and "will not be found liable in the absence of fault",[19]

---

15 *Id.*

16 *Id.*, at 140–41.

17 *Prodigy*, *supra* note 10, at 5.

18 *Id.*, at 3.

19 *Id.*

a publisher is held to a different standard. A "publisher" in defamation law is "one who repeats or otherwise republishes a libel"[20] and such a person is "subject to liability as if he had originally published it".[21]

While Cubby was appropriately regarded as a distributor in the previous case, Prodigy was held to have exercised editorial control over the harmful content. It made decisions as to content based on its guidelines, screening software, board leaders and their emergency delete function.[22] Even if it was no longer implementing all of these procedures, it had held itself out to the public as doing so, and had raised expectations that it was doing so.[23]

As in the *Cubby* decision, the court in *Prodigy* was mindful of the delicate balance between facilitating innovation in communications technology on the one hand and protecting existing legal rights to the protection of one's reputation on the other. It agreed with the posture taken in *Cubby* and reiterated that:

> Let it be clear that this Court is in full agreement with *Cubby* … . Computer bulletin boards should generally be regarded in the same context as bookstores, libraries and network affiliates. It is PRODIGY's own policies, technology and staffing decisions which have altered the scenario and mandated the finding that it is a publisher.[24]

The *Prodigy* court was also mindful of the apparent paradox its ruling was creating by holding that an online service provider that took *greater* care in managing content should be held to a greater standard of liability for doing so. It addressed the concern that such a holding would create a tendency for online service providers to choose to turn a blind eye to harmful online content for fear of attracting legal liability:

> For the record, the fear that this Court's finding of publisher status for PRODIGY will compel all computer networks to abdicate control of their

---

[20] *Id.*

[21] *Id.*

[22] *Id.*, at 5 ("PRODIGY has virtually created an editorial staff of Board Leaders who have the ability to continually monitor incoming transmissions and in fact do spend time censoring notes. Indeed, it could be said that PRODIGY's current system of automatic scanning, Guidelines and Board Leaders may have a chilling effect on freedom of communication in Cyberspace, and it appears that this chilling effect is exactly what PRODIGY wants, but for the legal liability that attaches to such censorship").

[23] *Id.*

[24] *Id.*

> bulletin boards, incorrectly presumes that the market will refuse to compensate a network for its increased control and the resulting increased exposure. Presumably, PRODIGY's decision to regulate the content of its bulletin boards was in part influenced by its desire to attract a market it perceived to exist consisting of users seeking a "family-oriented" computer service. This decision simply required that to the extent computer networks provide such services, they must also accept the concomitant legal consequences.[25]

This reasoning may be difficult to support in the absence of any empirical evidence as to the cost-benefits of launching a family friendly computer service. It seems a logical attitude on its face, but in the absence of clear economic evidence supporting the court's proposition, a risk remains that it will be less cost-effective for an online service provider to actively seek to protect users from harmful content. Particularly in cases where those who develop innovative communications technologies do not have the wherewithal or expertise to engage in a detailed cost-benefit analysis, the temptation would be to err on the side of less risk by taking less action to monitor content. It may be that the court made these comments to hedge its bets, knowing that in fact Congress would shortly deal with the problem in enacting § 230 of the CDA.

4.2.2 Section 230 of the Communications Decency Act

4.2.2.1 Publishers versus distributors under Section 230(c)

In the wake of decisions like those discussed in the previous section, Congress enacted § 230 of the CDA in 1996. The idea of the legislation was to clarify the position of online intermediaries in terms of their liability for content posted initially by a third party. These objectives are clearly stated in the statute. In particular, the legislation acknowledges that:

> It is the policy of the United States –
>
> (1) to promote the continued development of the Internet and other interactive computer services and other interactive media;
> (2) to preserve the vibrant and competitive free market that presently exists for the Internet and other interactive computer services, unfettered by Federal or State regulation;

---

[25] *Id.*

(3) to encourage the development of technologies which maximize user control over what information is received by individuals, families, and schools who use the Internet and other interactive computer services;
(4) to remove disincentives for the development and utilization of blocking and filtering technologies that empower parents to restrict their children's access to objectionable or inappropriate on-line material; and
(5) to ensure vigorous enforcement of Federal criminal laws to deter and punish trafficking in obscenity, stalking and harassment by means of computer.[26]

Congress intended to achieve these ends and, in particular, to encourage innovation in digital communications technology by limiting the liability imposed on intermediaries for content posted by third parties. The legislation even protects intermediaries who monitor and control third party content to some degree. Section 230(c)(2)(A) expressly deals with the *Prodigy* situation:

> No provider … of an interactive computer service shall be held liable on account – of … any action voluntarily taken in good faith to restrict access to or availability of material that the provider … considers to be obscene, lewd, lascivious, filthy, excessively violent, harassing, or otherwise objectionable, whether or not such material is constitutionally protected …

For these purposes, "interactive computer services" is defined in a way very similar to the broad concept of online intermediary discussed in this text. The statute defines "interactive computer service" as "any information service, system, or access software provider that provides or enables computer access by multiple users to a computer server, including specifically a service or system that provides access to the Internet and such systems operated or services offered by libraries or educational institutions".[27] Subsequent case law has applied this definition to Internet service providers such as America Online[28] as well as to more interactive online service providers such as an online roommate matching service.[29]

The main achievement of § 230, as far as online intermediaries are concerned, is the basic protection against liability for content created by others that is simply posted on an intermediary's website. Section 230(c) provides that: "No provider or user of an interactive computer service

---

[26] 47 U.S.C.A. § 230(b).

[27] 47 U.S.C.A. § 230(f)(2).

[28] See, for example, *Zeran v America Online*, 129 F.3d 327 (4th Cir. 1997); *Blumenthal v Drudge*, 992 F. Supp. 44 (D.D.C. 1998).

[29] *Fair Housing Council of San Fernando Valley v Roommate.Com*, 521 F.3d 1157 (9th Cir. 2008).

shall be treated as the publisher or speaker of any information provided by another information content provider". Before considering how this section has dramatically altered the position of online intermediary liability, it is worth making a few technical points about the operation of the legislation. Importantly, § 230(c) is not intended to apply to intellectual property law.[30] Thus, the safe harbor provided here for interactive computer services does not impact the safe harbor in § 512 of the Digital Millennium Copyright Act (DMCA).

At this point, it is also necessary to examine some of the statutory definitions of the terms used in § 230(c). The definition of "interactive computer service" is set out above, and the term "information" is left to its common meaning. However, the statute does contain a separate definition of "information content provider" the interpretation of which has proved central to judicial decisions involving § 230(c). "Information content provider" is defined in § 230(f)(3) as: "any person or entity that is responsible, in whole or in part, for the creation or development of information provided through the Internet or any other interactive computer service". The idea here is to clearly distinguish between intermediaries whose sole role is hosting, or providing a forum for the display of information, from those who actually create information.

What has proved challenging for judges is determining the point at which an online service provider who engages in some editorial control over harmful information should be regarded as the "creator" or "developer" of that information. That question has become an important one in light of the fact that early cases interpreting § 230 gave it a rather broad interpretation, creating almost a blanket immunity for online service providers even in circumstances where the service providers had some knowledge of the harmful material.

In *Zeran v America Online*,[31] for example, the Fourth Circuit was faced with a situation where an unidentified person posted a message on a computer bulletin board using America Online (AOL) as the Internet service provider. The posting stated that a number of items (such as t-shirts) containing offensive messages related to the Oklahoma City bombing could be purchased from "Ken" at the plaintiff's home phone number in Seattle, Washington. The plaintiff Zeran subsequently received threatening phone calls that included death threats. The posting was picked up by an announcer for an Oklahoma City radio station who encouraged listeners to call the number and threaten Zeran. Zeran

---

[30] 47 U.S.C. § 230(e)(2).
[31] 129 F.3d 327 (4th Cir. 1997).

complained to AOL who initially did nothing, but eventually removed the posting. Zeran sought, in the litigation, to hold AOL liable for defamatory content initiated by the unknown third party.

The court was highly deferential to the Congressional intention as stated in § 230 to keep the Internet free from intrusive government regulation and to maintain and encourage robust developments in interactive communications technologies.[32] The court noted that while the original poster of the message – to the extent that person could be located and brought to justice presumably – might be held liable for a defamatory posting, Congress had chosen to create a broad immunization from liability for online service providers such as AOL.[33] The judge was mindful of the staggering amount of information filtered through online intermediaries, stating that: "The specter of tort liability in an area of such prolific speech would have an obvious chilling effect. It would be impossible for service providers to screen each of their millions of postings for possible problems".[34]

In other words, faced with the balance of protecting existing legal reputational interests and technological innovation, Congress here chose to prioritize the latter. This is the same balance we have examined in other areas of law earlier in this book, notably in terms of the balance between intellectual property rights and technological innovations. However, in the case of harmful content regulation, Congress found a different balance, imposing a lesser burden on online intermediaries than in the case of intellectual property rights. The possible reasons for this divergence in approach are discussed below.

The court in *Zeran* was also mindful of the Congressional intent to encourage service providers to engage in filtering and protection of users of their services from harmful material.[35] The idea was to undo some of the damage allegedly done by the *Prodigy* decision in potentially

---

[32] *Id.*

[33] *Id.*, at 330–31 ("Congress made a policy choice … not to deter harmful on-line speech through the separate route of imposing tort liability on companies that serve as intermediaries for other parties' potentially injurious messages").

[34] *Id.*, at 331.

[35] *Id.* ("Another important purpose of § 230 was to encourage service providers to self-regulate the dissemination of offensive material over their services").

disincentivizing online service providers from engaging in such filtering for fear that they would be held to a higher standard of liability for so doing.[36]

In the face of the court's unwillingness to impose liability on an online intermediary for defamatory content posted by another party, Zeran raised an interesting argument, drawing from the pre-§ 230 discussions of defamation law. He argued that while § 230 may well have been intended to immunize a *publisher* from liability for content posted by another, it should not be read as immunizing a *distributor* from liability where the distributor had sufficient knowledge to make it liable. Harkening back to cases such as *Cubby v Compuserve*,[37] distributors (such as libraries and newsstands) would only be held liable where they knew or had reason to know of the defamatory material.[38] Zeran argued that once he had put AOL on notice of the harmful posting, it knew or had reason to know of the defamation and should be held liable as a distributor.[39]

Zeran further argued that because § 230(c) specifically refers to a "publisher," Congress must have intended to leave distributor liability intact for online intermediaries even in the wake of the legislation. He was here referring to the aspect of § 230(c) that states that the intermediary shall not be treated as a "publisher or speaker" of information provided by another. The court rejected this argument, stating that

---

36 *Id.* ("Congress enacted § 230 to remove the disincentives to self regulation created by the [*Prodigy*] decision. Under that court's holding, computer service providers who regulated the dissemination of offensive material on their services risked subjecting themselves to liability, because such regulation cast the service provider in the role of a publisher. Fearing that the specter of liability would therefor deter service providers from blocking and screening offensive material, Congress enacted § 230's broad immunity 'to remove disincentives for the development and utilization of blocking and filtering technologies that empower parents to restrict their children's access to objectionable or inappropriate on-line material'").

37 776 F. Supp. 135 (S.D.N.Y. 1991).

38 *Id.*, at 140–41.

39 129 F.3d 327, 331 (4th Cir. 1997) ("interactive computer service providers like AOL are normally considered … to be distributors, like traditional news vendors or book sellers. Distributors cannot be held liable for defamatory statements contained in the materials they distribute unless it is proven at a minimum that they have actual knowledge of the defamatory statements upon which liability is predicated … Zeran contends that he provided AOL with sufficient notice of the defamatory statements appearing on the company's bulletin board").

"distributor" is actually a subset of "publisher" and cannot be distinguished from it.[40] The court draws from defamation law in examining the relationship between the terms publisher and distributor, noting in particular that the foundational charge in a defamation case is "publication" whether as a creator of content or one who passes on that content without removing a harmful statement.[41] The court notes that the distinction between *publishers* and *distributors* in traditional defamation law relates to two different standards of liability and not to two different classes of potential defendant.[42]

Particularly relevant to the discussion of the future of cyberlaw, the court here notes that the creation of liability on notice to an intermediary would defeat the purpose of § 230(c) because it would reinforce the service providers' incentives to restrict speech and abstain from self-regulation.[43] This is clearly a different approach to intermediary liability from that taken in § 512 of the DMCA with respect to intermediary liability for copyright infringement. In § 512, intermediaries will be held liable for infringement if they do not act expeditiously once they are put on notice of an infringement by the copyright holder.

In *Zeran*, the court interpreted the Congressional intent behind § 230 of the CDA as not requiring an online intermediary to act even after it is put on notice of a harmful online communication. With respect to defamatory statements, the court stated:

> If computer service providers were subject to distributor liability, they would face potential liability each time they receive notice of a potentially defamatory statement – from any party, concerning any message. Each notification would require a careful yet rapid investigation of the circumstances surrounding the posted information, a legal judgment concerning the information's defamatory character, and an on-the-spot editorial decision whether to risk liability by allowing the continued publication of that information. Although

---

[40] *Id.*, at 332 ("Assuming … that Zeran has satisfied the requirements for imposition of distributor liability, this theory of liability is merely a subset, or a species, of publisher liability, and is therefore also foreclosed by § 230").

[41] *Id.* ("'[E]very one who takes part in the publication … is charged with publication.' … Even distributors are considered to be publishers for the purpose of defamation law … ").

[42] *Id.*, at 332 ("It is undoubtedly true that mere conduits, or distributors, are subject to a different standard of liability … . [D]istributors must at a minimum have knowledge of the existence of a defamatory statement as a prerequisite to liability. But this distinction signifies only that different standards of liability may be applied within the larger publisher category, depending on the specific type of publisher concerned").

[43] *Id.*, at 333.

> this might be feasible for the traditional print publisher, the sheer number of postings on interactive computer services would create an impossible burden in the Internet context.[44]

The concern for the court was under these kinds of circumstances, online intermediaries would have a "natural incentive to remove messages upon notification, whether the contents were defamatory or not".[45] This would create a significant chilling effect on freedom of online speech,[46] which would run counter to the government's policy in developing the Internet.

There are a number of ways the difference in approach between § 230 and that of § 512 of the DMCA could be explained. It may be that copyright claims are easier to verify and it was easier to put a workable "notice and takedown" regime in place for copyright infringement claims. It could be that copyright holders have more lobbying power than potential victims of defamation and other harmful online comment. The distinctions in approach between these two sections are taken up in more detail below.[47] However, it is first important to examine how judicial interpretations of § 230(c) developed subsequent to *Zeran*.

4.2.2.2 Judicial interpretations of "information content provider" under Section 230

For many years the leading case, and the most contentious, involving § 230 was *Blumenthal v Drudge*.[48] This case also involved America Online (AOL) as a defendant. AOL had entered into a license agreement with Matt Drudge, author of The Drudge Report, an online news aggregation site that originally started as a Hollywood and D.C. gossip site with a conservative bent. Under the license, The Drudge Report was to be made available to all AOL's members for a period of one year. In exchange, Drudge received a monthly royalty payment of $3,000 from AOL. The litigation arose with respect to an edition of the Drudge Report that contained allegedly defamatory material about the plaintiffs. The question for the court was whether AOL could be held liable for the defamatory content in light of the enactment of § 230 of the CDA.

Effectively the court's decision turned on its interpretation of the term "information content provider" as contemplated in the legislation in concert with the stated legislative intention to protect online service

---

44 *Id.*
45 *Id.*
46 *Id.*
47 See discussion in Part 4.3, *infra*.
48 992 F. Supp. 44 (D.D.C. 1998).

providers from liability for the speech of others. The plaintiffs argued that both Drudge and AOL should be held liable for the defamatory comments as joint "information content providers" under the legislation. Drudge was obviously an information content provider because he wrote the story in question, while the plaintiffs argued that AOL was also responsible because it had some role in writing or editing the material.[49] However, this argument was rejected on the basis that AOL did not actually edit any of Drudge's posted content.[50] The plaintiffs had also argued that Drudge should be regarded as an agent or employee of AOL and thus AOL should be liable for the publication on that basis. However, the court found no evidence to support this assertion either,[51] and noted that the plaintiffs ultimately seemed to have abandoned that line of argument.

Despite the difficulty faced by the plaintiffs in mounting an argument under which AOL would be held liable as an information content provider under § 230, the court seemed somewhat sympathetic to its plight. The court acknowledged that AOL here was more than the kind of passive conduit of information that it believed § 230 was enacted to protect. Here, AOL had contracted with and paid Drudge what amounted to the equivalent of a salary of $36,000 a year for their subscribers to have access to his column. They had reserved the right to remove, or direct Drudge to remove, content that violated their Terms of Service and to require changes to content that in AOL's judgment might adversely affect the operations of its network.[52] AOL had also issued a press release encouraging its subscribers to read the Drudge Report and describing the kind of material – gossip and rumor – they would be able to access through the Report.[53]

Finding for the defendants, the court expressed a dim view of AOL's activities, asking: "Why should AOL be permitted to tout someone as a gossip columnist or rumor monger who will make such rumors and

---

[49] *Id.*, at 50 ("plaintiffs suggest that AOL is responsible along with Drudge because it had some role in writing or editing the material in the Drudge Report").

[50] *Id.*

[51] *Id.* ("It is also apparent to the Court that there is no evidence to support the view originally taken by the plaintiffs that Drudge is or was an employee or agent of AOL …").

[52] *Id.*, at 51.

[53] *Id.* ("shortly after it entered into the licensing agreement with Drudge, AOL issues a press release making clear the kind of material Drudge would provide to AOL subscribers – gossip and rumor – and urged potential subscribers to sign onto AOL in order to get the benefit of the Drudge Report").

gossip 'instantly accessible' to AOL subscribers, and then claim immunity when that person … defames another?"[54] Ultimately, the court held that it is because of the operation of § 230 that the defendants must be held immune from suit:

> Congress has made a different policy choice by providing immunity even where the interactive service provider has an active, even aggressive role in making available content prepared by others. In some sort of tacit quid pro quo arrangement with the service provider community, Congress has conferred immunity from tort liability as an incentive to Internet service providers to self-police the Internet for obscenity and other offensive material, even where the self-policing is unsuccessful or not even attempted.[55]

This case was regarded by many as the high water-mark of § 230's impact on harmful speech online. It allowed online service providers of various stripes to claim complete immunity even when they had a hand in the content being disseminated via their services. One might argue that the result in *Drudge* was legally incorrect as a matter of statutory interpretation and that the court could just as easily have held that one who contracts with another to provide a particular kind of information should be regarded as an "information content provider" under § 230. The wording of the statutory definition of "information content provider" might appear broad enough for such a statutory construction. As noted above, "content provider" is defined in § 230(f)(3) as "any person or entity that is responsible, in whole or in part, for the creation or development of information provided through the Internet or any other interactive computer service".

While AOL clearly did not write The Drudge Report itself, its contract allowing it to edit entries available to its subscribers might be taken to suggest that it was "responsible in part" for the information at least in the form passed on to its own subscribers. However, this is not, strictly speaking, what the statute contemplates. For an entity to be regarded as an "information content provider", that entity must have been responsible for the *creation* or *development* of the information in question. While AOL had the ability to seek edits for unsuitable content, that did not amount to creation or development of the information in the first place, thus protecting it from liability.

---

[54] *Id.*

[55] *Id.*, at 52.

In the court's own words: "While it appears … that AOL … has taken advantage of all the benefits conferred by Congress in the Communications Decency Act, and then some, without accepting any of the burdens that Congress intended, the statutory language is clear: AOL is immune from suit …".[56] This result may also be regarded as an example of how difficult it is to draft clear legislative rules that deal with the rapidly evolving landscape of online commerce and communications. Even though the case arose in the early days of the Internet, rapidly in the wake of the enactment of § 230, it involved a situation for which Congress had not specifically thought to provide. Congress had in mind online service providers wrongfully facing liability for monitoring harmful content posted by others without their knowledge. Very soon, these very same service providers started contracting for content and found themselves able to hide behind the statute to avoid liability.

However, as noted above, in some ways *Drudge* was the high-water mark of the statute. Subsequent cases have considered the situation differently. Again, technology has changed and the resolution of § 230 cases will vary depending on the ways in which the technology is utilized. While AOL was able to avoid liability by relying on its lack of actual creation of information disseminated over its services for a commercial profit, the defendant in *Fair Housing Council v Roommate.com*[57] was not so lucky. This case involved an online service provider that operated a website to match people renting out spare rooms with people searching for housing options. It profited from its services from subscriber fees and advertising revenues.

Roommate.com required its members to create user profiles that involved answering basic questions including disclosure of gender, sexual orientation and whether he or she would bring children into the household. They also had to describe preferences in a roommate with respect to the same three criteria. Additionally, they were invited to add comments describing themselves and their ideal roommate in an open-ended essay format. The required answers were provided by way of drop-down menus where users clicked the appropriate response to each question while the essay comprised filling in a text field. The litigation arose when several Fair Housing Councils sued Roommate.com on the basis of violations of the Fair Housing Act and Californian housing discrimination laws which prohibited discrimination in providing housing

---

56 *Id.*, at 52–53.

57 521 F.3d 1157 (9th Cir. 2008).

on the basis of criteria including sex and familial status. Thus, unlike most of the previous litigation involving § 230, this was not a defamation action.

In terms of the § 230 issues, this case revolved squarely around the questions that confronted the court in *Drudge*. In other words, who should be regarded as the "information content provider" in circumstances where an online service provider has some involvement in the creation or development of allegedly harmful content? In *Roommate.com*, the court accepted, as the earlier court had accepted in *Drudge*, that an online service provider may be both an "interactive service provider" and an "information content provider" simultaneously under § 230 in certain circumstances: "If [the online service provider] passively displays content that is created entirely by third parties, then it is only a service provider with respect to that content. But as to content that it creates itself, or is 'responsible, in whole or in part' for creating or developing, the website is also a content provider".[58] In such a case, the online service provider will be liable for the content which it is partly responsible for creating, but not liable for content that is wholly created by a third party.

According to the court, the nature of the user profiles on Roommate-.com fitted the bill for information that was created partly by the defendant and partly by its members. Providing pre-populated terms in drop-down menus that users were required to choose made Roommate a developer in part of the content of the ultimate user profiles, even though the users themselves chose the terms that filled in their profile questionnaires:[59]

> By requiring subscribers to provide the information as a condition of accessing its service, and by providing a limited set of pre-populated answers, Roommate becomes much more than a passive transmitter of information provided by others; it becomes the developer, at least in part, of that information. And section 230 provides immunity only if the interactive computer service does not "creat[e] or develop" the information "in whole or in part" ...[60]

According to the Court, because Roommate made "answering the discriminatory questions a condition of doing business",[61] they were to be

---

[58] *Id.*, at 1162–63.

[59] *Id.*, at 1165 ("the fact that users are information content providers does not preclude Roommate from *also* being an information content provider by helping 'develop' at least 'in part' the information in the profiles").

[60] *Id.*, at 1166.

[61] *Id.*

regarded as partial information content providers with respect to the harmful information. The same reasoning applied to their roommate "search" function which was designed to rely, at least in part, on the discriminatory housing criteria. However, with respect to the personal essays incorporated into user profiles by users, Roommate was not regarded as an information content provider because it did not participate in the creation or development of the information other than by providing a text box within which users could complete the personal essay.[62]

In subsequent proceedings, the Ninth Circuit held that Roommate.com had not actually violated the Fair Housing Law with respect to its conduct.[63] However, the precedent relating to § 230 remains good law. To the extent that an online service provider actually engages in the creation or development of illegal information, say, through drop-down menus and pre-populated fields in forms, they may be regarded as an "information content provider" under § 230. This reasoning perhaps provides some consternation for providers of Internet search technologies that utilize "auto-complete" functions, such as when a user begins typing a query into a search engine and the search engine suggests terms the user might be searching for. As technology continues to advance, § 230 will doubtlessly be reconsidered in light of new ways in which an online service provider might be considered to be "creating or developing information".

Section 230 of the CDA is a good example of Congress attempting to strike a legislative balance between protecting existing legal rights and promoting innovative global communications technologies. As with all legislation – and common law – attempting to achieve this balance, the technology often outpaces the law at a rapid rate. With § 230, Congress clearly had in mind early online service providers who needed to be protected in their efforts to provide communication forums for huge user bases while avoiding liability for any particular comment made by an Internet user. However, developing commercial practices (*Drudge*) and technological developments (*Roommate.com*) soon outpaced the scenarios originally contemplated by Congress, leading to often unpredictable results in new cases.

---

[62] *Id.*, at 1173–74.

[63] *Fair Housing Council v Roommate.com*, 666 F.3d 1216, 1223 (2012) ("Because precluding individuals from selecting roommates based on their sex, sexual orientation and familial status raises substantial constitutional concerns, we interpret the FHA and FEHA as not applying to the sharing of living units. Therefore, we hold that Roommate's prompting, sorting and publishing of information to facilitate roommate selection is not forbidden by the FHA or FEHA").

Another interesting aspect of Congress' approach to online service provider immunity in § 230 is the contrast between this legislation and Congress' approach to safe harbors for copyright infringement in 17 U.S.C. § 512 which was enacted around the same time. A comparison of these provisions is instructive for a discussion of what a new conception of cyberlaw might contribute to the development of the law more generally. If cyberlaw was more focused on questions of intermediary liability for global communications, there would be a more obvious intellectual space within which to streamline approaches to similar challenges amongst different fields.

4.3 CONTRASTING INTERMEDIARY LIABILITY FOR DEFAMATION AND COPYRIGHT INFRINGEMENT

As discussed in the previous chapter, the safe harbor regime for online service providers with respect to copyright infringement is somewhat different to the approach taken under § 230 for other forms of legally wrongful speech. Under the copyright act, online service providers may face liability for content posted by others that infringes copyright if they do not act expeditiously to remove the material after being made aware of its posting.[64] The legislation also requires copyright holders to comply with certain requirements in serving a takedown notice on an online service provider to ensure that they do not use the notice and takedown procedure to engage in fishing expeditions in search of potential new defendants. Thus, the copyright provisions – under OCILLA[65] – strike a delicate balance between the promotion of technological innovation and the protection of existing copyrights. Copyright holders are required to go to some effort to monitor their protected content in cyberspace and when an infringement is discovered, they may enlist the aid of the notice and takedown regime in OCILLA. Online service providers must comply with the notice and are also required under the statute to notify the poster of the allegedly infringing material of the takedown[66] and be prepared to reinstate the material if it is non-infringing.[67]

With respect to defamatory content and other harmful communications outside the intellectual property sphere, § 230 of the CDA strikes a different balance with respect to online service providers, giving them

---

64 17 U.S.C. §§ 512(c)(1)(A)(iii); (c)(1)(3).

65 17 U.S.C. § 512.

66 17 U.S.C. § 512(g).

67 *Id.*

what looks almost like an absolute immunity from liability. The only exception is in a case like *Roommate.com* where the service provider in question actually *creates* content – in whole or in part. However, content posted by a third party, even if facilitated, contracted for, or encouraged by a service provider, will generally not meet this statutory requirement as in *Drudge*.

One might posit various reasons to explain the difference in approach to the liability of online service providers under the two statutory regimes, and it may be that each statute strikes the balance between protecting existing legal rights and promoting technological innovation in the most appropriate way for its content. However, what is missing from the debates in cyberlaw to date has been much in the way of comparison of the two regimes. There was little discussion of what each regime might learn from the other when the respective bills were drafted.

A more focused cyberlaw field could assist in the development of legislative approaches, and subsequent judicial interpretations of legislation, as it pertains to cyberspace communications. While the drafters of the CDA were focused on the protection of minors and others from harmful content and the drafters of OCILLA were focused on the balance of copyright interests against innovations in online services, there was little theoretical space in the 1990s for a comparison of the two. While both sets of statutory drafters were faced with a detailed consideration of the emerging role of online service providers and the impact of imposing significant legal burdens upon them for conduct initiated by others, there was little space or time to consider those commonalities.

The acknowledgment of a scholarly field within which to consider these questions of online intermediary liability would allow debates to be better focused on various practical and political issues that should be taken into account when enacting legal rules that will impact similar online intermediaries generally. As intermediaries ultimately need to adapt their own policies and practices to meet the requirements of all of these legal regimes, it would benefit them to know that there was a field of law in which their interests would take center stage in law reform debates.

With respect to the CDA and OCILLA, one might have these debates today and could easily reconcile the differences in legislative approach to online service provider safe harbors in a post hoc manner. For example, it is possible to argue that establishing copyright infringement is much easier to do in practice than establishing defamation or other harm from tortious speech. Most copyrights in the United States are registered and most copyright holders carefully monitor their interests online. Thus, it is more reasonable to ask an online service provider to act when confronted with a takedown notice from a copyright holder than with a complaint from an alleged victim of defamation or other harmful speech. The copyright notice is perhaps more likely to be objectively valid and can be supported in most cases by third party verification of registration of the copyright. On the other hand, requiring online service providers to act in the face of a notice alleging defamation or other harmful speech outside of the copyright regime would arguably put an impossible burden on those online intermediaries in terms of the potential for chilling online speech if they do act, or being held complicit in tortious conduct if they fail to act. Thus a more absolute immunity for defamation is arguably justifiable for online service providers than may be the case with respect to copyright infringement liability.[68]

While such justifications for the difference in legislative approach to safe harbors for online service providers make sense, they are nevertheless distinctions made largely after the fact. Little comparative discussion – certainly very little academic discussion – took place at the time of the enactment of the respective statutes, or in the years immediately following. A failure to engage in such comparative discourse potentially misses the synergies that could benefit the development of more harmonized laws from the online service provider's perspective. In both the case of copyright infringement and defamation, an online service provider is put in the position of having to make decisions about censoring content posted by others with the risk of being held liable for infringement if they fail to do so. The provisions of the CDA give such intermediaries much more comfort with respect to defamation than the provisions of OCILLA give them with respect to copyright infringements. Thus, online service providers are much more likely to act to remove information that is alleged to infringe a copyright than they are to remove allegedly defamatory content posted by others.

The need for an area of legal scholarship that focuses more squarely on the role of online intermediaries in a global context is not confined to intellectual property and defamation law. The role of the intermediary is implicated in other ways in cyberspace. An area that has come into the limelight in recent years is the protection of privacy and anonymity, particularly when online intermediaries hold increasing amounts of personal information about individuals and are often in the position to aggregate that information on a scope and scale never before possible. The following chapter considers the careful balance that needs to be

---

[68] Jacqueline Lipton, *The Law of the Intermediated Information Exchange*, 64 FLORIDA LAW REVIEW 1337, 1354–55 (2012).

struck by online intermediaries in collating, utilizing and safeguarding personal information in cyberspace. Global differences in approach to the legal protection of personal information emphasize that a cyberlaw focusing more on the obligations and rights of online intermediaries has an important international dimension that may also differentiate it from other existing areas of law.

5. Digital privacy and cyber-victimization

5.1 DIGITAL CHALLENGES FOR THE PROTECTION OF PRIVACY AND ONLINE VICTIMIZATION

Privacy law is a difficult field to pin down at the best of times and those difficulties are exacerbated in the digital age because of the ease with which personal data can be manipulated – aggregated, stored and disseminated. Scholars the world over have struggled to define the theoretical underpinnings of the field of privacy law. Privacy as a legal right has variously been conceived as a property or quasi-property right, a right related to personal autonomy, a right to protection of one's reputation somewhat akin to the defamation regime, and a right related to bodily integrity.[1] Cultures vary in the extent to which they seek to enshrine privacy as a constitutional right. One of the sharpest jurisdictional divisions in privacy law is between the European Union countries where privacy is incorporated as a fundamental human right in the European Convention on Human Rights,[2] and is reflected in large-scale privacy protection regulations,[3] and the United States where privacy is peripherally implied from constitutional provisions related to due process.[4]

Prior to the digital age, privacy laws tended to exist in the shadow of other fields of law, like defamation. However, the advent of global, instantaneous and inexpensive communications technologies brought

[1] Jacqueline Lipton, *Mapping Online Privacy*, 104 NW. U. L. REV. 477, 488–92 (2010) (surveying theories of privacy law).

[2] Convention on the Protection of Human Rights and Fundamental Freedoms, art. 8 (right to privacy); art. 10 (right to free expression).

[3] See, for example, Directive 95/46/EC of the European Parliament and of the Council of 24 October 1995 on the protection of individuals with regard to the processing of personal data and on the free movement of such data.

[4] See discussion in DANIEL SOLOVE, MARC ROTENBERG, and PAUL SCHWARTZ, INFORMATION PRIVACY LAW, 33–34 (2 ed 2006) (discussing implied constitutional foundations of U.S. privacy law).

privacy law to the fore as a field with which citizens the world over, and their governments, have to contend. Digital technology enables collection, aggregation, storage, recompilation and dissemination of personal information on a scope and scale never before imaginable, thus leading to concerns about the protection of individual privacy. In terms of the discussion in this book, it tends to be digital middlemen – including governments, academic institutions, online retailers, online advertisers, search engines and online social networks – that do much of the information collation and put personal information to useful or profitable use. Thus, the field of privacy law significantly implicates the activities of those engaged in the provision of innovative digital services, the focal points for this discussion of cyberlaw. Recently, Google has been effectively held liable in the European Union for generating search results involving temporally outdated personal information that may be harmful to individuals.[5]

Often, the online intermediaries that handle personal information are in contractual relationships with the information subjects. For example, Facebook as an online social network collects and collates much personal information from its members in order to use it in targeted advertising campaigns and the like. The digital movie library, Netflix, aggregates consumer preferences and compares them to those of other members with similar preferences in order to make suggestions of what customers might like to watch. Digital retailer Amazon.com does the same with all manner of products. In cases where the online service provider has a contract with its members, it can incorporate privacy policies within its Terms of Service, and many service providers do just that. Additionally, where the service – such as an online social network – enables members to post information about others, the Terms of Service/Privacy Policies may incorporate rules or suggestions about the importance of not infringing other people's privacy and not sharing personal information without permission.

However, plenty of online service providers utilize an individual's personal information without the benefit of a contract that governs the uses they may make of the information. Of course, it should be noted that even where a contract is in place, it is usually drafted by the online service provider and thus will focus on that party's interests rather than those of the consumer-members of the service. To the extent that members' interests – or the privacy interests of others – are taken into

---

5 *Google Spain v Costeja González*, Case C-131/12, Court of Justice for the European Union, May 13, 2014.

account in the Terms of Service, the enforcement of contractual rights is generally at the discretion of the service provider, as is the ability to alter the terms unilaterally.[6]

In cases where no contract is in place, privacy protections are at the general discretion of the online service provider, subject only to legal rules that may apply in a given jurisdiction. For example, the Google search engine uses personal information to better target search results to individual searches, and some of the information it generates has been held legally harmful.[7] There is no contract between search engine users and Google, and its algorithms for targeting search results – and advertising – are proprietary to Google, so the recourse for those concerned about privacy incursion is limited to general laws which vary significantly between jurisdictions.

None of this is to say that information aggregation technologies should be discouraged. Many individuals benefit greatly from the technological innovations employed by Google, Facebook, Netflix, Amazon and many other online service providers. While some people may be uncomfortable when Amazon or Netflix gives them suggestions of what other products they might be interested in based on past purchasing habits, or the purchasing habits of like-minded customers, others may appreciate the services. Thus, privacy is difficult to regulate effectively because even within a particular jurisdiction, opinions may diverge significantly on the benefits versus detriments of particular uses of personal information.

In fact, privacy harms are notoriously difficult to identify and even more difficult to quantify in legal terms. If a company uses my personal information to target advertising toward me or to tell my friends I purchased a particular item, what damages have I suffered? As some scholars have pointed out, the actual damage may be the creation of a culture of unease and a sense of being watched rather than an actual quantifiable loss.[8]

The more obvious cases of privacy-related damage for which the law is perhaps better suited as a regulator arise where a private fact is publicly disclosed on a website and that fact causes ongoing personal humiliation and perhaps loss of employment, insurance, or academic opportunity. Even the ready disclosure of outdated public facts can have a similar result. The appropriate remedy here may be an injunction against the

---

[6] Jacqueline Lipton, *"We, the Paparazzi": Developing a Privacy Paradigm for Digital Video*, 95 Iowa Law Review 919, 921–22 (2010) (providing examples of online vigilante justice) [hereinafter, *Paparazzi*], at 975–76.

[7] *Id.*, at 936–40.

[8] *Id.*, at 948.

website to remove the information, which is something the law can deal with very easily via court order where the relevant substantive laws are available. Such was the case in the action against Google in Spain for removal of harmful personal information from search results.[9]

However, despite the plaintiff's success in protecting his personal information in that case, there is no American law that would achieve a similar result. Thus, the protection of one's reputation in the way achieved in the European Union is arguably not available in the United States. Once something is posted online in the United States, the genie is effectively out of the bottle and there will be little legal recourse for any individual harmed by online disclosures of personal information, unless the information is false and harmful, grounding a defamation action.

Another privacy law area that has involved online intermediaries arises in cases where an anonymous individual's identity is required to be disclosed in the context of legal proceedings. This is an area which implicates online service providers greatly because often a service provider is the only party who can identify a potential witness or defendant to litigation where that person has posted anonymously. Several cases have arisen in the digital age where courts have been asked to formulate approaches to determine in what circumstances an online service provider should be required to disclose personally identifying information about one of their member-customers in these circumstances.[10] By and large, this task has not been too difficult as it is based on expectations of fairness and due process. People are generally aware that even if they contract with a service provider for anonymity, that anonymity may be pierced in cases where a court requires disclosure.

An area closely related to privacy regulation that will also be discussed in this chapter is the area of cyber-victimization generally: including cyber-bullying, cyber-harassment and cyber-stalking. These fields of law raise similar challenges to privacy in the digital age because they all concern an individual's ability to be autonomous online without threat of damage to their personal integrity or reputation, or fear for their physical safety as a result of online communications. Additionally, in the United States in particular, the regulation of such conduct raises significant challenges for judges and legislators because of the powerful First Amendment protections for online speech. This is one reason why the

---

[9] See note 5, *supra*.

[10] See, for example, *Columbia Ins v SeasCandy*, 185 F.R.D. 573 (N.D. Cal. 1999); *In re Subpeona Duces Tecum to America Online Inc*, 52 Va. Cir. 26 (2000); *Doe v 2TheMart.com.*, 140 F. Supp.2d 1088 (W.D. Wa. 2001); *Doe I and Doe II v Individuals whose true names are unknown*, 561 F. Supp.2d 249 (2008).

European Union's privacy regulations have not been replicated in the United States.

While some cyber-victimization laws in the real world have been supported constitutionally because of the real threat of physical harm to the victim,[11] much online conduct can be more problematic as it may not be clear or likely that physical harm will come to an individual as a result of online communications.[12] It can be notoriously difficult to predict when and whether anonymous or pseudonymous online communications support a concern about real world harm to an individual and, if so, who the likely perpetrator of that harm would be.

Another similarity between cyber-victimization and privacy violations is that in the United States at least the regulation of these areas of conduct tend to be left to often disharmonized or ineffective state laws and are not covered in any detail at the federal level. Because the Internet crosses jurisdictional boundaries, the reliance on disharmonized state laws is problematic for effective enforcement of regulations on acceptable online conduct. The same is true for defamation laws and fair housing laws, the kinds of issues discussed in the previous chapter.

The above survey of the contexts in which privacy and associated concerns are implicated in online communications evidences that privacy law is a large field with amorphous boundaries, made even more amorphous and difficult when the conduct occurs in cyberspace. A book chapter on digital privacy can do little more than scratch the surface of the issues facing those seeking to regulate online privacy. However, a discussion of the area is important in the context of reconceptualizing cyberlaw because privacy law is one of those areas which emphasizes the need to create a regulatory approach for online conduct that focuses on digital intermediaries and their activities on a global scale. The fact that Google is forced to comply with a radically different privacy regime between the United States and the European Union is an obvious example of this disparity.

While it is unlikely that a global consensus on the protection of individual privacy values will be achieved anytime soon, a regulatory approach that focuses squarely on the role of online intermediaries and baseline expectations as to the protection of individual privacy will assist in the development of the policies and practices employed by those entities in the future. Such an approach may also highlight synergies that

---

[11] Jacqueline Lipton, *Combating Cyber-Victimization*, 26 BERKELEY TECH L. J. 1103, 1126 (2011) [hereinafter, *Cyber-Victimization*].

[12] *Id.*

arise between policies and procedures employed to protect privacy with those employed to balance the protection of intellectual property rights in personal reputations addressed in previous chapters.

5.2 ONLINE SERVICE PROVIDERS AND THE REGULATION OF PRIVACY AND CYBER-VICTIMIZATION

Unlike the other areas described in this book, the regulation of privacy and cyber-victimization raises different regulatory pressures for online service providers than intellectual property. This is because privacy and victimization laws (harassment, stalking, bullying) are relatively underdeveloped in the United States in particular as compared with those other bodies of law. Until 2014, it was not clear that search engines had a legal responsibility under the European Union privacy regulations to protect individual data. The position in the United States is even less clear, except to the extent that it may be believed that there are no such obligations under American law.

For example, while there have been instances of the Federal Trade Commission entering into consent decrees with websites to regulate what the websites do with personal information of individual users, the bulk of the pressure on online services to protect privacy comes from customers themselves. The consumer backlash toward Facebook's Beacon Advertising Program a few years back is a great example of this.[13] The protection of customers' privacy rights on web services tends to involve a delicate dance between the service providers who seek to utilize the information to provide more tailored services and targeted advertising, and customers who feel the need for stronger controls over how their information is used.

As noted in the previous section, when the online service in question is a service that enters into a contractual relationship with a customer as a condition of membership, privacy rights and responsibilities can be incorporated into the Terms of Service. Whether or not the consumer reads those terms and whether or not the service provider is vigilant about enforcing them is often a matter of discretion. However, a contract can be a solution in terms of *providing* the rights in the first place in jurisdictions like the United States with little in the way of effective privacy law. Of course, there is a lack of bargaining power on the

---

[13] Lipton, *Paparazzi*, *supra* note 6, at 973–74.

consumer side in the contract law context, but assuming some competition in the marketplace for the relevant service (which is not always the case[14]), there might be sufficient pressure on the service provider to at least create some level of privacy protection for customers.

Even with respect to online service providers who contract with their members to protect privacy, the contractual privacy policies are not easily enforceable by third parties whose privacy rights are infringed by those utilizing the service. Thus, if I am a Facebook user/member and you are not, I can write about you on my wall in a way that you feel has infringed your privacy or has victimized you in some other way, but you will have little recourse. I may have infringed my contract with Facebook, but you would have to convince Facebook to take action against me in line with the terms of my contract with Facebook.

The prevention of cyber-victimization is particularly problematic in this context. The legal regulations to prevent online harassment, stalking and bullying are quite weak in the United States[15] and many of them may be held unconstitutional if challenged.[16] The victims of online harassment may suffer significant emotional harm, but will not have any contractual recourse against those who have engaged in the harmful communications.[17] Additionally, as noted in the previous section, the kinds of emotional harms suffered by the victims of this kind of conduct are difficult for courts to quantify,[18] even in cases where there is a legal cause of action available to the victim. Where the emotional pain leads the victim to harm herself, the damage may ultimately be very real and truly horrific but the law is not well situated to provide recompense.[19]

As noted with respect to the recent CJEU ruling involving Google search results, the position on the protection of individual privacy and the protection of one's reputation and autonomy online is very different in the European Union to the position in the United States. Since the dawn of the information age, the European Union has maintained high levels of

---

[14] For example, if all my friends are on Facebook, I'm unlikely to use a different social networking service even if there are other services available.

[15] Lipton, *Cyber-Victimization*, *supra* note 11, at 1116.

[16] *Id.*, at 1128.

[17] This is particularly problematic where a person harmed is not a party to the contractual terms of service of a particular website.

[18] See, for example, discussion in Jennifer Meredith Liebman, *Defamed by a Blogger: Legal Protections, Self-Regulation, and Other Failures*, 2006 U. ILL. J.L. TECH. & POL'Y 343 (2006).

[19] See, for example, discussion in Lipton, *Cyber-Victimization*, *supra* note 11, at 1121–22.

privacy protections that apply to individuals, businesses, governmental agencies and others who maintain personal information digitally.

Rather than relying on market-forces and certain sector-specific regulations as is the case in the United States, the approach to protection of personal information in the European Union has been all-encompassing and has imposed obligations on those who handle digital information to deal fairly and transparently with it. The European Union has continued to strengthen and bolster its regulatory stance and is revitalizing its already powerful protections to take better account of developments in digital technology since the implementation of its original regulations. The year 2014 sees the unveiling of the new privacy regulations in the European Union.[20] These regulations effectively bring the United States potentially further out of step with the E.U. Member States in terms of protecting digital privacy.

The protection of individual privacy online thus raises a number of important issues in the context of developing a cyberlaw framework for the future. This area squarely places law reform and legal regulation up against other modes of regulation such as social norms, market forces and system architecture in the digital age. It may be that privacy and associated concerns about online victimization are areas better suited to other regulatory modalities, particularly in the United States where the First Amendment might prove a serious impediment to powerful privacy regulations by Congress or the courts. However, that is a question that needs to be debated, particularly in light of the increasing disharmonization at the international level about privacy protection online generally.

Online intermediaries should be encouraged to consider their role in preventing harmful online conduct outside of areas where they are concerned about the likelihood of legal penalties. It may be that their motivation comes from market forces and social norms in the area of privacy and cyber-victimization rather than from the threat of legal regulation, although the CJEU decision requiring Google to delete certain information from its search results is a move that may at least motivate other online intermediaries to take more care when handling personal information.

Governments should also be aware that in order to effectively protect privacy in the digital age they may have to think creatively about how to regulate in order to protect individuals from harm from privacy breaches.

---

[20] European Commission – MEMO/14/186 12/03/2014, available at http://europa.eu/rapid/press-release_MEMO-14-186_en.htm, last viewed on June 30, 2014.

Some privacy harms are more tangible than others. For example, identity theft as a result of a privacy breach may be more easy for a government to address, at least in legislative terms, than emotional harm as a result of a cyber-bullying campaign, although most victims of identity theft would attest to the difficulty of redressing the harms actually suffered.

5.3 A SURVEY OF PRIVACY AND CYBER-VICTIMIZATION REGULATION

Before leaving the discussion of privacy protections in the online world, it is worth examining some of the American privacy laws to consider whether the government can or should do anything consistent with the First Amendment and the needs of online communities to bring the laws more in line with the realities of online communications. The obvious starting place is the four privacy torts recognized in the Restatement (Second) of the Law on Torts. These torts are the basis for most civil privacy protection in the United States. They were developed in the mid-twentieth century and are sorely out-of-date in the context of digital communications.[21] The privacy torts are set out in §§ 652A–E of the Restatement. They may be summarized as: intrusion upon seclusion;[22] appropriation of name or likeness;[23] publicity given to private life;[24] and, false light publicity.[25]

The shortcomings of these torts in protecting privacy rights in a digital world have been well documented.[26] However, in summary, the main issues with these torts are that they are largely based on a combination of physical world conceptions of public versus private spaces, and that they focus on fairly egregious individual privacy incursions. These foundations for privacy law do not translate well to digital settings where the predominant concerns are often aggregations of small amounts of data rather than large one-off privacy breaches.

The intrusion upon seclusion tort is highly charged with physical world constructs, and is only infringed where a defendant has encroached on another's reasonable expectations of privacy usually with respect to

---

[21] See, for example, discussion in Patricia Sánchez Abril, *Recasting Privacy Torts in a Spaceless World*, 21 HARV. J.L. & TECH. 1 (2007).

[22] Restatement (Second) of the Law on Torts, § 652B.

[23] *Id.*, § 652C.

[24] *Id.*, § 652D.

[25] *Id.*, § 652E.

[26] Sánchez Abril, *supra* note 21.

physical space.[27] Thus, spying into someone's living room and taking photographs of private conduct may infringe the tort, but hacking into another person's Facebook page probably would not meet the requirements of intrusion into seclusion as currently conceived.

The tort that prohibits the unauthorized use of someone else's name or likeness would likewise have little useful application in cyberspace where most of the privacy incursions are related to aggregations of personal data for targeted advertising purposes and the like. The creation of an algorithm to ascertain that if customers A, B, and C liked product X, Y, or Z so it can be marketed to other customers with similar spending and demographic profiles to A, B, and C is not really an *appropriation* of customer A, B, or C's name or likeness as conceived in the Restatement.

The misappropriation tort as currently drafted is aimed at false endorsements or uses of pictures of private individuals in advertising campaigns without their consent.[28] It is possible that a message generated by Facebook and sent to Betty telling her that her friend Alice enjoyed a particular product could infringe the tort. In this case, Facebook would actually be using Alice's *name* to endorse a product. So there are some online circumstances where the tort may have teeth, but those situations are probably in the minority of online privacy concerns.

The public disclosure of private facts and false light publicity torts have both been interpreted by courts to apply to fairly egregious and offensive public disclosures of private information.[29] They would certainly not apply to the use of data aggregations for targeted advertising purposes. They may apply in certain cases of cyber-victimization where disclosures about an individual are highly embarrassing or humiliating. However, the Internet may take away as much as it gives here. Defendants facing a claim under either tort would likely argue that online conduct has had a disinhibiting effect over time, and has desensitized us

---

27 Lipton, *Paparazzi*, *supra* note 6, at 959–60.

28 *Id.*, at 960.

29 Restatement (Second) of Torts § 652D (1977); ("One who gives publicity to a matter concerning the private life of another is subject to liability to the other for invasion of his privacy, if the matter publicized is of a kind that (a) would be highly offensive to a reasonable person, and (b) is not of legitimate concern to the public."); § 652E ("One who gives publicity to a matter concerning another that places the other before the public in a false light is subject to liability to the other for invasion of his privacy, if (a) the false light in which the other was placed would be highly offensive to a reasonable person, and (b) the actor had knowledge of or acted in reckless disregard as to the falsity of the publicized matter and the false light in which the other would be placed.").

to offensive content.[30] In any event, cases of public disclosure of private facts and false light publicity were very difficult to prove in the physical world, and are likely to be even more difficult to establish online both because of the disinhibiting effect of online communications and because many of the privacy incursions in cyberspace do not relate to individual disclosures, but to data aggregation and unauthorized use in targeted marketing campaigns.

Additionally, in the few scenarios where an online intermediary is potentially liable for infringing a privacy tort, that intermediary would have the additional legal protection provided in section § 230 of the Communications Decency Act. In circumstances where the online service provider was not actually itself the "information content provider" it would escape liability under the safe harbor. In a case like the hypothetical above where a social networking service uses the name of one of its subscribers to advertise a product to that subscriber's contacts, the service would likely be the information content provider, so would not be able to avail itself of the safe harbor. However, in most other situations involving a privacy tort, where it was actually information posted by a third party that was the subject of the action, the service provider would likely escape liability under § 230.

The American position on privacy may usefully be contrasted with the European Union position where the initial Data Protection Directive was aimed at regulating those who actually process and aggregate information. The new regulations continue in the same vein, and strengthen existing regulations.[31] The European Union approach is to place the onus on those who process and utilize large amounts of data about individuals to protect that information, provide transparency about their uses of the information, correct errors in the information, and receive consent to process particularly sensitive classes of information. The recent CJEU decision clarified the fact that search engines are regulated under the European Union data protection legislation as data controllers.[32]

Outside of the law related to privacy incursions per se, some criminal and tort laws are aimed at the results or harms that may be caused by sharing an individual's private information online or by targeting an individual as the focus of a verbal attack. These are the laws that might

---

[30] See, for example, SHERRY TURKLE, ALONE TOGETHER: WHY WE EXPECT MORE FROM TECHNOLOGY AND LESS FROM EACH OTHER, 235–36 (2011) (describing the way that individuals often respond to each other in much more coarse and aggressive ways online than in physical space).

[31] See note 20, *supra*.

[32] See note 5, *supra*.

be referred as cyber-victimization regulations. They pertain to engaging in conduct that either puts an individual in fear for her safety, or embarrasses or humiliates a victim, either because of who she is, or because of her membership in a particular class (for example, women, minorities etc.).[33]

These laws are problematic to draft in the physical world and even more so as they relate to cyberspace. This is because laws that aim to curtail speech, even potentially harmful speech, have the First Amendment to contend with in the United States.[34] Additionally, it is very difficult to draft a law that prohibits speech that is actually harmful while protecting speech that may be distasteful or unpleasant, but does not cause anyone major emotional or physical harm. It is impossible to draft a law forbidding a person to say anything about anyone online because that is plain censorship and would have a deleterious chilling effect on speech. However, the question of where and how to draw lines between speech that is actually harmful and dangerous in a cyber-victimization sense, and speech that is not, is incredibly challenging in practice. The task of effective drafting is made even more difficult by the disinhibiting effect of online interactions.[35] Speech that in the real world may cause a person to fear for her safety or to face serious emotional distress may have a lesser impact when communicated online. What is acceptable conduct online is often different to what would be accepted in a physical conversation.

Nevertheless, the harms engendered as a result of online communications can be – and have been – catastrophic in some cases. Several well-publicized instances of cyber-bullying, for example, have led victims to commit suicide.[36] In these cases, prosecutors have struggled with finding a law to fit the crime.

Most cyber-victimization laws are modeled on their "real world" precursors – laws relating to bullying, harassment and stalking in the real world. Traditional bullying and harassment laws tended to focus on communications targeted to cause a victim emotional distress,[37] while stalking laws have tended to focus on creating an apprehension of physical violence to the victim.[38] The latter is obviously more difficult to translate to the online context. In the absence of a physical threat of, say,

---

33 Lipton, *Cyber-Victimization*, *supra* note 11, at 1107–12.
34 *Id.*, at 1106.
35 TURKLE, *supra* note 30.
36 Lipton, *Cyber-Victimization*, *supra* note 11, at 1121–22.
37 *Id.*, at 1108–10.
38 *Id.*, at 1111–12.

someone following or approaching the victim in real space, it can be very difficult to establish the threat with respect to purely online communications. In terms of criminal laws, prosecutors may not be comfortable expending resources on cyberstalking if they have little experience as to how to prosecute the cyber-analog to physical world stalking.[39]

With respect to bullying and harassment, these laws are perhaps easier to translate or apply in an online context because in both cyberspace and the physical world, they revolve around communications that create emotional distress to the victim. Of course, bullying in the physical world often also comprises physical action. It is perhaps easier to think of someone as a bully if they have physically accosted the victim and threatened them, rather than in cases where they have simply communicated something verbal without any accompanying physical action. So this is another area where laws applied in the physical world may fall short of being helpful to victims in cyberspace.

Questions have also arisen about the extent to which these kinds of laws are constitutional, particularly when the defendant's conduct revolves around pure speech rather than threats of actual physical violence.[40] Again, prosecutors may be loathe to expand the resources on cyberspace prosecutions if they are unsure about how the existing laws might apply to online conduct, or when there are concerns about where any new laws drafted with cyberspace conduct in mind would survive a constitutional challenge by the defendant.

Again, as with much online conduct, it may be difficult in cases of cyber-victimization to establish who and where the defendant really is. If online harassers are operating anonymously or utilizing pseudonyms, it can be difficult to ascertain the real person behind the conduct without the assistance of the online intermediary or intermediaries through which they are communicating. In the infamous cyber-bullying case resulting in the suicide of teenager Megan Meier, the perpetrator of the bullying was in fact the mother of one of Meier's classmates, disguising her identity online under the fake persona of a young man who pretended to like Meier only to say horrific things to her that arguably resulted in her taking her own life.[41]

While online intermediaries will not be liable for harmful content posted by others because of the operation of § 230 of the CDA, cyberlaw

---

[39] *Id.*, at 1117–18.

[40] Lyrissa Barnett Lidsky and Thomas Cotter, *Authorship, Audiences, and Anonymous Speech*, 82 NOTRE DAME L. REV 1537, 1590 (2007).

[41] Lipton, *Cyber-Victimization*, *supra* note 11, at 1117–18.

discussions in the future should focus on the role played by intermediaries within these kinds of cases. Online intermediaries are in a unique position in that they can disclose the identities of defendants in cyber-victimization cases. Laws must be developed to ensure that intermediaries know when and how they are required to do so. Additionally, some thought needs to be given in this context to the extent to which different kinds of intermediaries should be legally required to monitor online conduct to ensure the absence of harmful conduct or at least to act in the face of complaints about damaging communications. While § 230 more or less immunizes online intermediaries from any liability with respect to cyber-victimization where the intermediaries themselves are not content providers, those online service providers may have little to no incentive to self-police.

Future cyberlaw debates should draw on lessons learned in other areas of law – intellectual property, defamation, fair housing and the like – to ensure that an appropriate balance is struck between protecting intermediaries from unreasonable liability for the conduct of others, while promoting established individual rights. This is something a reconceptualized field of cyberlaw can contribute to future debates. It can create a scholarly field within which to comprehensively discuss the role of online intermediaries on a global scale with respect to different categories of harmful conduct.

6. Conclusions on the future of cyberlaw

In many ways, this book has raised a lot more questions than it has answered, but the main question has been whether maintaining a distinct "cyberlaw" field, at least in academic discourse, is worth the candle. Hopefully, the author has presented a compelling case that the answer is "yes", particularly if the field can be refocused as contemplated in this text. While early cyberlaw theorists focused on the broader questions about what cyberlaw might entail and whether cyberlaw can, or should, illuminate the entire law in order to justify its existence, subsequent history has suggested that there may be other valuable contributions to legal academia and law reform to be made within the field.

The recent history of legislation and case law surrounding the Internet suggests that questions involving the nature of cyberlaw are more nuanced than initially supposed. Rather than focusing on regulation of "the Internet" per se, cyberlaw is – or should ideally be – concerned with the regulation of digital communications enabled by online intermediaries on a global playing field. The organizing principles for cyberlaw are found in this statement. Cyberlaw is at its heart the law of *digital intermediated information exchange*. Accepting this definition allows scholars, commentators, and others to focus on what may be learned by studying cyberlaw, notably about the central role played by the intermediaries that facilitate information exchange and the levels of liability that may reasonably be attached to them for communications often initiated by others.

A more comprehensive and unified approach to the role of intermediary regulation would help both those engaged in providing online services and their regulators determine, across many categories of conduct, the acceptable best practices for these entities. Thus, cyberlaw should cut across many existing fields of law including intellectual property, defamation, privacy, identity theft, fraud, cybervictimization, and other areas that are focused largely on information exchange. Contract law will be implicated to the extent that intermediaries can utilize contracts to monitor their users and prevent wrongful communications.

However, cyberlaw should not be – as Frank Easterbrook suggested – a cyber "law of the horse". It should not be a general consideration of a series of disparate legal fields to the extent that Internet communications are implicated at all under this varied set of torts, crimes and contractual principles. Rather, the focus should be largely on the role of online intermediaries within these various fields. When considering the role of online intermediaries, a careful balance must be struck between the promotion of innovation by these entities and the need to protect existing legal rights (including intellectual property rights, rights to privacy and protection of reputation). The field of cyberlaw must be geared to strike this balance by ensuring that online intermediaries do what is reasonable to prevent cyber-wrongdoing while at the same time avoiding the placement of costly and impossible burdens on these entities that would chill innovative practices.

To date, these questions of balance have been considered largely on an ad hoc basis within each disparate area of law. What might be gained by refocusing cyberlaw on these challenges more generally is a more comprehensive law of the online intermediary that takes account of the synergies between the challenges facing these entities across different bodies of law. It would undoubtedly be more helpful for a scholarly space to exist in which questions of the liability of intermediaries for a variety of online wrongs can be considered in a more comprehensive and organized manner. This is the contribution a refocused cyberlaw field could make. Ultimately, it would benefit the development of innovation in digital technologies if those service providers that faced similar challenges could have scholars and lawmakers consider those challenges in a more synergistic way.

The cyberlaw field should also maintain a clear focus on the idea of regulating *information exchange*, as distinct from physical activity. Everything online is a communication rather than a physical action. As we saw in the previous chapter, some laws revolving around physical world harms, like stalking, simply do not translate well to the online context. Where a legal field is premised on the exchange of information, specific legislative challenges arise in jurisdictions such as the United States with its powerful First Amendment jurisprudence protecting free exchange of information from government interference. The protection of free speech must always take a relatively central role in any organized study of cyberlaw because all of cyberlaw is at its heart about the exchange of information between individuals facilitated by online service providers.

The global nature of the Internet, while not included in this book as a central tenet of a new cyberlaw field, should also remain an important consideration for cyberlaw scholars. While jurisdictional problems will continue to arise in Internet-based litigation, the global nature of online communications raises other specific regulatory challenges. For example, cultural differences will pose regulatory problems depending on the extent to which one considers that a law of the Internet should be globally harmonized. While, say, intellectual property laws are relatively well harmonized internationally, laws relating to defamation, privacy and cyber-victimization are less well-harmonized. Many of these laws are in fact not well harmonized within any given jurisdiction. The advantages and disadvantages of disharmonization should be part of future cyberlaw debates and discussions. Advantages of international disharmonization of laws as they relate to cyberspace include opportunities for international arbitrage and the ability to compare different regimes as they deal with similar practical issues. Disadvantages of disharmonization include lack of certainty for litigants as to outcomes and, in fact, appropriate forums for judicial determinations related to online conduct, which can lead to increased expenses for all parties and in some cases can lead to the lack of a potential remedy. For example, in *Chang v Virgin Mobile*, the plaintiff effectively had no legal remedy available when the Texas court refused jurisdiction over the case because the appropriate forum (Australia) did not maintain substantive laws relating to unauthorized misappropriation of an individual's name or likeness.[1]

Another way in which the reconceptualized cyberlaw framework suggested in this book differs from previous debates about the area is that while the author advocates a consideration of law as simply *one* of a number of potential regulatory modalities for cyberspace conduct, she also suggests that law remains an important part of the regulatory arsenal. Previous scholars such as Professors Lessig and Reidenberg have suggested that code, rather than law, is the most effective regulator of online conduct and what debates about Internet law perhaps teach us is the importance of focusing on code as a more effective regulator.[2] While agreeing with the view of the power of code – as well as social norms and market forces – as online regulators, the author suggests that it is nevertheless important not to lose focus on law as an important form of regulation of online conduct. As all of the different regulatory modalities overlap and intersect in complex ways, it is important to study all of them to ensure a full regulatory picture. Thus, law must not be demoted from

---

1 U.S. Dist. LEXIS 3051 (2009).

2 LAWRENCE LESSIG, CODE 2.0 (2006); Joel Reidenberg, *Lex Informatica: The Formulation of Information Policy Rules through Technology*, 76 TEXAS L. REV. 553 (1998).

the mix. Additionally, as other scholars have pointed out, even where law serves more of an expressive or social guidance function, that role can be as important, if not more important in some cases, as relying on law as an enforcement mechanism.[3] Even laws that may ultimately prove unconstitutional express governmental concerns about appropriate online behaviors.

While this book has focused selectively on certain areas of law to make the case for reconceptualizing cyberlaw as the law of the intermediated information exchange, it has done so advisedly. It has taken as examples the central areas of much scholarly debate and legal jurisprudence involving the Internet in the last 15–20 years and has identified synergies that have been missed between the regulation of copyrights, trademarks, defamation, privacy and the like, particularly with respect to the role of online intermediaries. Presumably there are other areas that could have been discussed. However, the author focused on those areas that have caused the most media attention and that have come to the fore in cyberlaw casebooks and syllabi.

The aim of this book has been to draw attention to ways in which cyberlaw could be reconceived as a more cohesive and useful field for the future. The idea is to ensure that scholars, legislators, and judges be aware that there is a place for a true *law* of the Internet (in concert with other regulatory modalities identified above). The true benefits of such a field may not have been fully appreciated in the past because of the focus on specific legal problems rather than a broader retrospective view as to what has taken up the most time of judges, legislators and cyberlaw scholars since the explosion of the Internet in the 1990s. Cyberlaw can be a much more important scholarly field than it has been in the past. It can be a field for gathering together common threads of conduct relating to intermediated online information exchanges. Hopefully this book has provided a useful step in the ongoing debate toward developing a cyberlaw that contributes something more useful to the future evolution of legal principles as they apply to online conduct.

---

[3] See, for example, Danielle Keats Citron, *Law's Expressive Value in Combating Cyber Gender Harassment*, 108 MICH. L. REV. 373, 404 (2009) (discussing the "expressive role" law could play in the area of cyber gender harassment).

Index